OLD EUROPEAN PEWTER

A. J. G. VERSTER

OLD EUROPEAN PEWTER

with 118 illustrations

THAMES AND HUDSON · LONDON

© J. H. DE BUSSY, AMSTERDAM 1957

THIS EDITION © THAMES AND HUDSON LONDON 1958

PRINTED IN THE NETHERLANDS

CONTENTS

PREFACE

Nullus est liber tam malus ut non aliqua parte prosit

'No book is so bad as to have no value at all', provided that the subject is of interest. But does this apply to yet another book about old pewter—a subject which has been dealt with by quite number of distinguished English writers, who have sung the praises of the pewterer and his products?

Most of these books, however, describe English pewter, so it might still be opportune to add to them another book on Continental pewter ware.

This book has no claim to being a scientific treatise. In any case it would not be possible to write an exhaustive account in the allotted space; though I have aimed at giving a maximum of variety. For more information, I would like to refer the reader to the authors listed in the Bibliography.

These chapters are no more than 'talks' about pewter, merely sketches to accompany the illustrations. A great number of early specimens are represented, as I feel these to be the most characteristic types. I think collectors will agree with me that, unlike ourselves, pewter becomes more beautiful with age, thereby heightening our appreciation of the early examples.

In fact the older the piece, the more it is cherished by its owner. I have included many of the old flagons, as these represent, better than any, a large variety of styles and forms.

I wonder if we have ever realised how great is the diversity of these simple utensils which were in daily use. Do they not offer us more than the wine they contained? Do not their sturdy shapes convey to us something of the nature of our ancestors?

Is there not a glimpse of Latin grace reflected in the French cymaise, or an impression of authority emanating from the monumental flagons, used by the city fathers to refresh themselves while dealing with the business of governing their town? The Plates were selected and executed with the purpose of illustrating the development of the old craft through the centuries.

I have avoided placing the examples against a plain white background. In giving them more intimate surroundings and a livelier setting, I have attempted to recreate the atmosphere in which these antiques were originally used. I hope that these photographic reproductions of a pewter collection may stimulate those who wish to study the subject from the canvasses and panels of the Old Masters. The changeable climate of Northern Europe made people value comfort inside their homes, as can be seen in the still lives and interiors of the painters. When contemplating the works of the old painters one realises how much the robust and sober pewter, in all its simplicity, enriched the beauty of the home.

There is no doubt that the artisans were concerned, first and foremost, with producing a practical article. But their unerring judgement of proportions, their unspoilt feeling for style and line, led to such logical and well-balanced results that their simple trade became an art. So it is, that the form of an object can sometimes give us a better conception of the people and of a period than many a printed word.

PEWTER IN HOME AND TAVERN

Qui sedet post fornacem
et habet bonam pacem . . .

IT IS NOT FOR AESTHETIC
considerations only that I have given such ample space in this
book to the actual appearance of pewter-ware, for I know very
well how criteria differ, but my aim is to illustrate also how much
the language of its form tells us of the background of our for-
bears.

In order to understand this relation more clearly we must
first picture in our minds the interior of their homes.

In the Middle Ages religious art strongly influenced all types
of dwellings. Decorative motifs, tracery and arches, were all
developed from ecclesiastical architecture, the construction
itself dictating the particular form. Fine oak was used for the
simple, easily moved furniture. Loose table tops on trestles,
benches, folding chairs, stools, all made of wood, as were the
chests and trunks with their iron fittings. Only the beds and
cupboards were built into the walls. The dresser of the period
is often seen in contemporary paintings. The rooms had high
beamed roofs and often a floor of green and yellow tiles. The
white stucco walls were panelled or hung with tapestries, and
through high windows a subdued light filtered into the room.
The fire, originally in the centre of the room, was subsequent-
ly moved to a side wall, with a hole for the escape of smoke.
Later a chimney was built on the outside wall; the next improve-
ment was a heavy wooden beam over the fire-place and still
later a cowl with profiled supports on either side was construct-
ed. Terracotta tiles were built in round the fire-place and there
was an iron plate at the back. The fuel was burnt on fire-dogs
or in an iron basket, and from a pot-hanger or hook hung a
kettle.

The influence of the Renaissance was not apparent in the Low
Countries until the 16th. century. Then the constructive style
I have mentioned made way for one of more elaborate shapes,
a somewhat heavy and uninspired style at first, which soon

became lighter and more graceful in line. Arabesque ornamentation, acanthus leaves, medallions, mythological motifs, Grecian and Roman vases, arches and pillars, in fact every conceivable form of classical decoration was used. Of particular importance was the work of Vredeman de Vries with his fantastic models and ornaments, his excessive scroll-work and grotesques. This experimenting with line and form, though admirable, lacked the Gothic grandeur and majesty, whose soaring lines were replaced by a horizontal style. The arrangement of the home was so far the same, with a wall partially dividing the front from the back of the house. The dresser was replaced by a side-board, chests were replaced by cupboards, and chairs were used instead of benches; but the beds were still in the living quarters. The hood over the fire-place was now supported by pilasters or caryatids.

A greater variety of form and colour in the interiors was introduced during the 17th. century. The chairs were upholstered with leather or velvet. Pewter dishes or tankards stood on the side-board and the lights were reflected in the shining ball of the brass chandelier. The rich patrician families had floors of marble and walls of gilt leather. Great wealth was lavished upon sumptuous interiors and magnificent designs. In the Low Countries interiors were as yet subdued and less ostentatious. Later, however, the columnar table legs swelled into giant bulbs, the panels of the cupboards blew out as thick as cushions, heralding the arrival of the Baroque period.

The 18th. century brought refinement, but also a craving for more abundant luxury. This found expression in the veneers and inlaid decoration, the use of exotic woods, richly chased silver-ware, delicately coloured Eastern porcelain, and precious glass work.

In the first half of this century more and more curved lines appeared until with the Rococo style every straight line became a curve or spiral. In the Netherlands at this time the pewterers slavishly copied the designs of the silversmith.

Throughout these centuries many painters found the interior of the home an engrossing subject. On their canvasses they depicted the rich colours of Persian carpets, the deep blue and brown of earthenware, and the gleam of copper, pewter and glass on polished oak. One thinks of the still life paintings of that vivid character Pieter Claesz, the quiet, grave Willem Claesz Heda, van Ostade, Frans Hals, Buytenwech and many others. Which of their 'school' painted the still life against the cool monochrome background on Plate I? It is not painted by anyone. The well-known Viennese collector R. M. Vetter arranged this 17th.century group, added a 20th.century lemon and photographed the familiar combination.

Pewter depicted in pictures of the time has been discussed by D. F. Lunsingh Scheurleer in *Oud Nederland* (1950) and H. H. Cotterel and R. M. Vetter have written on this subject in *Antiques* (1929). We are struck by the beauty of the old interiors and furniture shown in these pictures. Some are rather overpowering, but most of them show quite simple taste. Which brings me to the beautiful simplicity of our pewter.

The Dutch pewterer, notwithstanding the great variety in the forms of his products, gave them the simple line which did not violate the nature of his material, but on the contrary enhanced its good qualities, and with many an old piece we are enchanted by the infallible taste of these simple artisans. In early pieces we occasionally find the influence of wood, bronze, or earthenware prototypes.

For comparison it is also useful to mention products from other countries.

The British pewterers did not indulge in excessive ornamentation either: they produced many pure and simple articles, but in less variety than their colleagues on the continent. In England there used to be less interest in continental pewter than in its own product. The English 'regular' still enjoys his pint in a pewter tankard, and collectors have got together and formed a 'Society of Pewter Collectors'. The alloys used by the English pewterer were sometimes rather hard, and thus the surface of the objects, in the course of time, did not always acquire the patina which is one of the charms of old pewter.

In Germany, on the other hand, the material used was often too soft, containing a high proportion of lead, which resulted in a dull finish. One finds there a preference for large pieces of opulent design, often at the expense of the proportions of the finished work.

It is too ornate for our taste, even where the outline remains unspoilt, and years of cleaning and polishing have sometimes worn down the soft metal to such an extent that much of the decorative work has been lost.

Despite these facts, however, some German and French craftsmen have created real masterpieces of the so-called 'Noble Pewter': the most important being a Frenchman, François Briot. In France these works of art were called 'Orfèvrerie d'étain', and in Germany 'Edelzinn'; some were also made in Austria and Hungary. This particular type of pewter work was not made for every day use in the home, but was meant to be kept as ornamental decoration. In the great German collections, some of which I have noted in the Bibliography, and in the museums of Cologne, Leipzig and Dresden, most distinguished decorative pewter can be seen. But this work misses the simple beauty of such plain pieces as the famous tankards produced during the late Middle Ages, mostly in the Hanseatic towns.

In Scandinavia, pewter articles have been found which were obviously copied from the old wooden table utensils; one is reminded here of the wooden bands round the old coopers' barrel, the pierced wood work etc.

Although certain characteristics help us to ascertain the country of origin of pewter, it is often very difficult to form a definite opinion and a series of interesting articles on this subject have been written in the American journal *Antiques* with the help of R. M. Vetter. Distinctive features may indicate the place of origin, even the specific town where the article was made, but as members of this guild suffered an inherent form of wanderlust, special shapes or finishes were transferred from one town to another, and even over the borders from country to country.

Pewter was used in the household many centuries ago, and has even been found among Roman and Greek remains. The oldest piece reproduced in this book is a Roman vase (Plate I). More examples from this era can be seen in the British Museum. Then followed a long period from which no pewter has been preserved. Much later, in the year 1284, we find pewter articles listed in the accounts of the town of Dordrecht. The oldest tankard pictured here (Plate II) carries in relief on the inside of the base the date 1331. In his work *Etudes sur l'etain* M. G. Bapst describes the methods of casting and working early pewter.

It was not until the 16th. century that pewter was used on a large scale in the home. The exploitation of the tin mines made it cheaper, and its special advantages became generally recognised. The protective oxydised surface was quite harmless and made it a suitable container for liquids; it was unbreakable, simple to clean, and above all it was easily moulded and shaped. It had a warm homely look, far less imposing than the more valuable silver, which turned black so quickly. The ordinary folk of the land displayed pewter as silver was set out in the homes of the rich, it became in fact 'the poor man's silver' and they often owned an adequate quantity for their food, and, more important still, their drink. Pewter was also used for the official banquets of the city fathers, and as they celebrated together, so their soldierly guards gorged themselves, beer and wine flowing abundantly.

During the 17th. century this soft gleaming metal maintained its place in the homes of the people, and whereas we have very little 16th. century pewter (in the Rijksmuseum, Amsterdam, there are some interesting relics of the Nova Zembla expedition), many 17th. century examples can be found in museums and collections.

Should there be no date-mark on the pewter it is risky to decide upon its period by considering only the shape and style, because the expensive bronze moulds from which it was cast were handed down from one generation to another. It was therefore possible that the products of a foundry retained the same forms for centuries, as these heavy moulds were set aside only with the greatest difficulty. Collectors and dealers are apt to back-date any black and aged piece, calling it Medieval. It is safe to assume that pieces found among the ruins of a building which was actually 'sacked', were made previously to the date of the destruction.

In the course of the 18th. century, silver-ware designs were copied in pewter. This was not a great success, as models were produced which were not in harmony with the essence of the soft medium used. Then towards the end of the century the character of the metal was completely lost in a covering of paint. As the pewter was hidden under a layer of paint, the alloy was less carefully prepared, and among the coloured pewter much material of very poor quality was sold. This was the beginning of a period of decadence for the noble guild, since the strength or weakness of a craft depends largely upon the actual craftmanship.

In addition, porcelain, earthenware and glass made their appearance and gradually took the place of pewter. Jan Luyken in his *Reflections on the work of the Craftsman* (Spiegel van het Menselijk Bedrijf) has written these lines on pewter-ware:

> A pewter spoon you cannot miss,
> A platter or a serving dish,
> These useful things are cheap and neat,
> For broth and bread, for fish and meat.

Not only were the contents of the pewter-ware enjoyed, but the containers themselves were highly valued in home and tavern. But painted on an 18th. century porcelain plate is the following unkind little verse:

> Pewter plates are not so good,
> Since they must be polished,
> If porcelain plates are on the wood,
> This work can be abolished.
> Set out, therefore, if you're able
> Porcelain plates upon the table.

And thus, like most earthly things, pewter had its rise and fall, its glory and oblivion. It was banished from the livingroom to the kitchen, where the servant sold it to the rag and bone man. Only a few workshops were able to maintain their trade for long. The firm of Meeuws & Son in the Hague, which has been in existence for over 200 years, has a great number of old bronze moulds still in use. The original old tools and diestamps are still used and all the work is done by hand as in the olden days.

What are the reasons for the fact that, despite the numberless bronze casting moulds which have been in use in the Low Countries, relatively little antique pewter from the earlier centuries has been found?

We have already pointed out that preference was given to

certain new materials. Of course much has been destroyed in times of wars and unrest. Fortunately the German 'Edelzinn' (noble pewter) which I have mentioned earlier was often spared because of its artistic value, as Dr Berling wrote: 'Dass dies auch für die Kunst der Zinngieser wirklich bedeutungsvolle Stücke betroffen habe, glaube ich kaum, denn dazu war die Denkmalpflege in den einzelnen Deutschen Ländern zu sehr auf dem Posten'. ('I find it difficult to believe that many really important pieces of 'Edelzinn' have been destroyed, as the Government used to keep a keen watch on their preservation.')

Sometimes pewter has been spared for a different reason, for instance by the plunderers of Alkmaar who, we are told by the chronicles of 1517, left all the pewter behind. 'Yes, the pewter was not of sufficient value to be worth taking with them'.

The greatest enemy of antique pewter has been the melting pot. Pewter householdware was considered to be of less value than that of costlier metals, and when it was slightly damaged, or out of fashion due to the introduction of a new style, it was hastily rejected or thrown into the melting-pot.

Travelling pewterers journeyed from one village to another, recasting the articles made of this soft metal, so easily damaged. In their repair work they made lavish use of lead, which was a dishonest method and brought them into disrepute among members of the guild. They were incapable of repairing any but the most simple pieces, and as a result of their work many of the earlier examples disappeared completely. At one time laws were made prohibiting the repair of damaged pewter, and pre-scribing recasting since this was usually much easier than actual repairing. Some of the pewter-ware was also melted down and used as a soldering material. If left dry on a fire, pewter melts immediately. It is well known that much pewter disappeared from the churches during the Reformation and ensuing disso-lution of the Monasteries.

When the ruins of Rotterdam were being cleared after the 1940 bombing, a number of early pewter pieces were brought to light from among the foundations. Here they had been buried for centuries in a type of soil which had left the metal unscathed. A few of these specimens are to be seen in the collection of H. J. E. van Beuningen and the Boymans Museum, both in

Rotterdam. On the other hand examples which have been dug up in other parts of Holland are mostly so damaged by chemical action and corrosion, that they are practically worn away. This seems to be the case in England also, as the well known British expert, the late H. H. Cotterell, reports: 'Not a single duly authenticated piece of English pewter of earlier date than the 16th. century is kown to exist'.

Much pewter has been lost to us through a disease which we call 'pewter pest', a contributory reason for impaired or damaged fragments being found in excavations. The disease attacks the metal in spots, which bulge and cause the metal to crumble into a grey powder, leaving a rough cavity which cannot be removed.

There are two forms of tin, the one used in pewter alloys is a white coarse crystalline metal. At temperatures below 13° C. it changes into a gray powder consisting of smaller crystals with a greater specific volume. This change shows as a sort of swelling on the surface of the pewter, which bursts and disintegrates, leaving unsightly holes. It is also contagious, thereby making the name 'pewter pest' even more apt. Grey tin in a diseased piece, brought in contact with a healthy specimen, will infect it and accelerate the rate of disintegration. Some impurities in the metal used by the pewterers seem to stimulate this condition, while conversely a high lead content retards the process. It is kown that the addition of such metals as bismuth and antimonium reduces the rate of decay, and these have been the saving of much of the antique pewter we still have. It must not be stored in a cold place, or be allowed to come in contact with infected pieces. Hence the warning from Professor E. Cohen: 'Pure specimens shown in exhibitions are likely to disintegrate more quickly than would happen otherwise'.

In normally heated rooms the progress of this disease is so slow that no radical change could be observed in pieces which were infected several decades ago. Pewter exhibited for years in cold museums is likely to deteriorate far more quickly. To avoid confusion we could call the disease 'Museum pest', reserving the term 'Pewter pest' for the illness which affects susceptible people when they associate with fanatic collectors. Yet another property of this metal was its medicinal quality, which provides us with another link between pewter and swellings. Powdered pewter was used as a remedy for boils; but as many pewter alloys contain lead, the patient who took this medicine in the form of pewter filings stood a good chance of getting lead poisoning.

Now we will pass on from powder to pewter again. Dishes and tankards appear in the forefront of all collections of old pewter, as they did on the tables of our forefathers. Just as hunger and thirst are always with us, so banquets and revelling had their place throughout the centuries.

Many paintings of laden tables, before or after a meal, show us that the necessities and pleasures of life were combined with eating and drinking. 'Happy is he who finds peace by the homely fireside', or as Jan Luyken writes in his *Philosophy of Home Comforts* (Het leerzaam Huisraad):

> For all the tables laden gaily
> With flowing wine and tasty food
> Where man and wife are meeting gaily
> In quiet and in peaceful mood.

A study of these paintings teaches us much social history also, as each table is representative of its particular period. They show us the primitive life of the late Middle Ages, the rough meals of the 16th. century citizen, the sumptuous board of the rich 17th. century merchants, and the refined splendour of the French Grand' Epoque in the 18th. century.

The ordinary utensils on the 15th. and early 16th. century table did not match and were not arranged in any particular order, nor did the way in which people sat at table take any set form. Sometimes spoons are evident on the table, but forks did not then exist. The solid food was eaten with nimble but greasy fingers, which were afterwards wiped on the table cloth, or on the communal napkin spread over the knees. Alternatively they made use of a large copper or pewter basin and ewer, not a superfluous measure considering how they ate their meal.

The guest cut his meat with his own knife, on a slice of rye bread or on a flat wooden trencher. In the 15th. century this primitive platter was replaced by a pewter one of similar shape.

Plate 42 shows the type of 16th. century round pewter platter. In addition, pewter was used for the numberless jugs and mugs, and for the indispensable salt-cellar.

The stately bulbous-legged table of the 17th. century was usually covered with a damask cloth and looked more interesting and colourful. Besides the cutlery, there was a great variety of scoured pewter, and in the centre stood the fish or poultry on a large pewter dish known as the 'Cardinals dish' (see plates 45—48).

In the 18th. century we find pewterware being gradually ousted by Chinese porcelain, Delft ware, Venetian or Bohemian glasswork, and rococo candelabras.

Now, where is the motley company gathered round the loaded tables? The soldiers and citizens, the yeomen and peasants, the courtly gentlemen and their ladies? They came and went with the years, the centuries. Immortality is granted to no one. The wine has been quaffed, the songs have been sung. Some paintings, some domestic ware, remain. But just as we hear the murmur of the sea in a shell, so, when all is quiet and still at home, an old pewter tankard echoes the past with nostalgic memories of wine and song.

The appearance of these tankards themselves suggests the wholesome spirit of their users and makers. Looking at the paintings which portray the hustle and bustle of a banquet, the roistering and revelling, we are struck by the firmness of the sturdy tankards and flagons. They were more fit for our solid citizens than the fastidious fluted glass or fragile porcelain.

We therefore honour these stalwart tankards by reproducing many illustrations of them in this book.

For the seasoned collector, always on the look-out for older relics, the 'Hanseatic' flagons provide a fascinating search. There are two definite types, the low thick-set model (plate 11) and the tall slender form (plate 14).

Attention was first drawn to these rare specimens by Professor Lauffer in *Spät Mittelälterliche Zinnfunde* and also by Professor Kratzenberger of Charlottenburg in *Altes Norddeutsches Zinngerät*. Miss M. A. de Visser has published an article on *Three Hanseatic Tankards* from Groningen in *Oud Nederland*. Writing about these in the American journal *Antiques* R. M. Vetter expresses the opinion that these compact heavy types were specially made for use on board ship as they would not topple over so easily. This theory explains, perhaps, why most of these flagons have been found in waterways in the locality of old wrecks. Opinions differ as to their country of origin, but they were definitely not exclusive to Northern Germany. The marks on the three 16th century Groningen flagons leave no doubt as to their origin. The tankard on plate 11 bears the year 1331, which is considered to be the earliest date ever found on pewter. Plate IX shows another 14th century flagon. In the museum at Flushing there are two specimens of this sturdy type of tankard which were found in the River Scheldt.

Like most of the early tankards, the 'Hanseatic' flagons were cast in two vertical sections. The lid is spherical with a slightly raised centre, a single hinge and a spectacle-shaped thumbrest. In later specimens the thumbrest is shaped like two acorns. The hinge is attached to the lid by means of a wedge-shaped extension. Another characteristic is the heavy handle which is triangular in cross section, decorated with ornamental foliage in relief on the flat outer side. The early types have a handle which is fixed to the top of the flagon, it then slants down slightly and curves into a deep bend before being attached in a vertical line to the lower bulge of the flagon. The short broad base on which it stands tapers sharply in a straight line.

Sometimes there is a medallion inside the bottom of the flagon, or on the lid, which was supposed to be a kind of charm or talisman to ward off evil spirits. Illustrations of these medallions can be seen on Plates 12 and X. They were sometimes considered to be the prototype for the 'Edelzinn' which was produced much later.

The characteristic form of the thick-set 'Hanseatic' flagon has never been repeated again, though the homely, powerful Gouda flagon on Plate 21 may perhaps be one of the same stock. Because of its tremendous weight it no doubt constituted a striking argument in a strong hand raised to settle a dispute in the tavern.

In North German museums there are some splendid Medieval goblets. Designed in the shape of a bronze mortar they have three seated lions at the base, two round handles, and a frieze in Gothic minuscules.

Another interesting type is the 's'Hertogenbosch' tankard (Plate 20). A small squat tankard bearing the municipal coat of arms of s'Hertogenbosch (Plate II), or, as on Plate 20, the crest of some other town. Quite often there is a medallion in the bottom of these tankards too. A large number are owned by the 'Illustrious Fraternity of Our Lady' or the 'Swan Friars', a society still in existence which counted among its members both William the Silent and Franciscus Sonnius, the first bishop of s'Hertogenbosch.

The late K. Azijnman, a s'Hertogenbosch collector, published details about these old pewter treasures in *Oude Kunst* 1918—1919.

In the same journal he also wrote about the Nijmegen Guild-flagons. These were used at meetings of the Guild in that town. Inscribed on them was the name of the particular guild to which they belonged, with occasionally the names of the masters. Verses and drawings were often engraved round their sides. Most of them have a round shield on the belly, and the lid has a tower-like protuberance. A Shoemakers' Guild tankard is reproduced on Plate 31, a Shippers' Guild on Plate 32, and on Plate 33 is a flagon belonging to a local fraternity. Despite their lavish engravings these flagons have a simple appearance compared with the monumental examples of the German Guilds. On Plate 31 we see the 'Wilkomm' goblet, hung with the silver shields of the Joiners' Guild, and the taped jug of the Butchers' Guild, a 'Schleifkanne', or flagon with sloping sides, which can be filled with beer and pushed across the table from one to another. The flagon of the Cologne Bookbinders' Guild on Plate 34 is less ostentatious.

The height of these flagons is an indication of the enormous thirst of these craftsmen. The early examples, with flat sides and rich decoration, sometimes fetched high prices. In 1909 the famous 'Breslau Zinnhumpen' was sold to the Berlin Kunstgewerbe Museum for 33000 gold marks. These Guild flagons are often heavy in stature, a quality they shared with those who drank from them.

The slender French wine tankard on Plate 38 is certainly more graceful. It has two handles, one fixed on the side and the other hinged over the top, reminiscent of the Gothic style. In similar, though bigger flagons, the municipality used to offer

III

IV

wine to their guests of honour, who were then allowed to keep the 'cymaise' or 'cimarre' flagon. Early examples of these beautiful flagons can be found in Swiss and French museums. Sometimes, as on the later Wallis flagons, a chain takes the place of the hinged handle.

In many a town-hall stands the huge 'Town Hall' flagon, D. F. Lunsingh Scheurleer describes Dutch specimens in chronological order in the 1944 volume of the *Archeological Annual*. As a rule the components of these flagons are easily recognised. They comprise a cylindrical or flat globular trunk with a long neck, standing on a high foot, and the lid usually has an elaborate top. The stucture of the early types shows Gothic influence. They were used on official occasions, or just stood as a decorative ornament. They were also used in the manner of the French cymaise, filled with wine they were sent to the house or inn where the distinguished guests were lodged.

Most collections possess a 'Rembrandt'' tankard; rather an extraordinary name for these 17th century flagons, since Rembrandt never painted the furniture of his time. Identified by a cylindrical widening at the neck and a somewhat narrowed foot (Plates 22 & 23) they are beautiful examples of structural harmony.

The contours of the later types were less definite, and in the 18th century the forceful baluster shape disappeared. During this period flagons with conical and cylindrical shaped trunks were also made (Plates 19 & 33).

In countries other than Holland similar flagons of varying styles were found, Flemish, French, German flat-lidded jugs, and the Scottish 'Tappit hen' which has no foot, the curving top-half developing into a vertical straight line to the base.

Extraordinary drinking vessels used at the meetings of the Guilds in Germany and Austria were designed to illustrate the craft they were representing. Examples of these are a shoe (Plate 75), a fish, a shuttle, etc.

Some German types called 'Stitzen' have a beaklike spout (Plate 27). In some cases this is designed like a man's face and is called a 'Fratzen'. The lidded tumblers with a handle (Plate 36) termed 'Rörcken' often have a pair of dice in the base.

The Dutch wine flagons with a long slanting spout closed

with a small lid are extremely rare (Plate I). They have been named 'Jan Steen' flagons, after the master who so often included them in his paintings. From these distinguished flagons a steady stream of wine was poured into the green glass rummers.

This type of flagon is also found in Switzerland, but there it invariably has a connecting bar, shaped like an arm or baluster, between the trunk and the spout. The lower part of the handle goes straight down, and the lid has a decorative knob (Plate 30). Writing about these flagons Vetter says 'Dutch ideas, possibly following the course of the Rhine, have provided the inspiration for several spouted flagons. The existence of this Dutch influence in Switzerland seems beyond all trace of doubt'. Plate 30 shows a French spouted flagon, and Plate 44 a German one with a large carrying ring on the screw lid. This last type, with a round or octagonal trunk, was commonly used in Switzerland for fetching the wine up from the cellar. E. Naef states that up to the present day the larger types of these 'Glockenkannen' are used to measure out the wine. 'Chaque année à un jour determiné, l'on se rend dans les caves de la bourgeoisie et l'on a droit de recevoir dans l'antique kanne d'étain à la belle forme de cloche la mesure de vin qu'elle contient'.

The Dutch 'Lambs Flagon' on plate 29 also has a connecting arm between trunk and spout. It is said that these little jugs were used for feeding lambs, but is it more probable that the drink in them was similar to that in the 'Jan Steen' flagons, and destined for stronger stomachs than that of a lamb. It is, however, also possible that they were used for invalids.

Additional characteristics to those already mentioned which help to date a tankard are the thumb-pieces. These vary according to the period and country of origin. Sometimes they are erect, or they curve back towards the handle, in other cases they are cloven, or shaped like two balls, acorns, masks, a feather, a shell etc. The English ones are sometimes rather elaborate. The 18th century German thumb-rests are nearly all globular, while the Scandinavian ones are rounded with a flat top and base.

Plate 39 shows a classic vase-shaped ewer with no lid. An example resembling this model has been found on the island of Nova Zembla in the Arctic Ocean, a relic of the expedition led by Heemskerk and Barendsz in 1596—1597. Its shape is reminiscent of the famous 'Temperantia' flagon made by Briot, but this one is engraved. The Nova Zembla ewer sets a problem—is it 'Edelzinn' of Dutch origin? The plaquettes cast in relief which were found in the same place might give reason to suppose that the ewers came from some other foreign source, yet, on the other hand, this type of ewer is frequently seen on Dutch paintings. R. M. Vetter has also found other evidence of its Dutch origin. In his article on *Silent Witnesses of the Nova Zembla Expedition* (Stille getuigen van de overwintering op Nova Zembla) B. de Kock assumes that the leaders had taken these specimens with them for use as barter. The numerous pewter candlesticks discovered on the island closely resemble the Dutch brass 'collar' candlesticks, differing only in their decorative work.

We will now mention some other types of flagon quite briefly. The octagonal flagon on Plate 9 is remarkable for its multilateral construction and typically Gothic contours. The rare flagon on Plate 10 with a handle and lid is actually shaped like the early bottles on Plate 3. The next reproductions show the characteristic vertical section structure of the early flagon. This is also noticeable in the specimen on Plate 15, with its somewhat 'ceramic' shape and in the one on Plate 16 with its typically French silhouette.

Plate 17 shows a group of 16th century prototypes of the Rembrandt flagon and on Plate 18 are two specimens which accentuate its familiar lines even more clearly.

The two Amsterdam flagons on Plate 23 and 24 are typical of the town where they were made—with their honest and straightforward bearing. Two curiosities on Plate 25 are the diminutive flagons, their smallness being emphasized by the vague silhouette of the large flagon behind. Plates 26 and 27 show how great a variety of small objects was in existence. The tankard on Plate 35 is an example of fine decoration in relief, while the one on the fore front of Plate 36 has much coarser relief work; both are products of the so-called 'noble pewter' work.

After this parade of flagons and tankards we feel we must leave this subject, or it will be too much for even the most fanatical tankard collector.

Perhaps I may be allowed to mention the measures, large and small, which were also produced in these shapes. Though they have no lid, there is usually a thumbrest on the top of the handle. In flagons and measures we often find one or more little pegs fixed on the inside, which mark the exact cubic measurements. The tall frothing mug was passed round, each drinker lowering the beer to the next peg; those in training were able to quaff a pegful in one draught. With the lowering of the beer there was a hightening of merriment—but in those days nobody seemed to be any the worse for that. To illustrate this I quote a passage on the subject by the old Flemish writer Mommaert:

When I have drunk so much that I can no longer maintain my balance, my servant guides me home and puts me to bed as he has been instructed. Once in my bed I usually sleep the whole night through, without care or torment, aches or pains, tossings or turnings. Hardly awake on the morrow, someone or other will invite me to accompany him to this or that tavern, where they say the best wines or beer are served. I dress hastily to join him at once, only half dressed, or uncombed and unwashed I arrive in the tavern. The landlady receives me, the company welcome me, and mine host calls 'Hola—give the squire a chair with a cushion, and hand him a draught from the new barrel we tapped yesterday'. And so we carry on as if we had never stopped. I am never at a loss for good company, there are many more of my ilk.

> Similis gaudet semper similis
> Birds of a feather flock together

Eventually I become drunk again—or as one might say, I am merry with drink—then I go away to sleep as I did the night before. I never have anxious or bad dreams, never notice the buzzing of gnats or biting of fleas. When I awake I find a good bowl of brandy beside my bed. From this I take a spoonful or ten or twelve, to liven up my stomach. The remainder is for my good friends who generally come and visit me during the morning. In this way I spend my time, doing harm to nobody, causing no trouble; which I think is a good and peaceful life. Nor do I notice or upset myself over the unkind gossip of my acquaintances who say that my way of life is not like a human, but like a pig. This is a lying and public slander, for whereas a pig always lies up to his neck in his own muck, and gulps his stinking food just to fill up his guts, I have other occupations. Not the least of them is joining my companions, who always concoct some new entertainment to the joy and delight of all. When the drink is in a man, he hears what never happened, he sees what has never been seen, and he who is always silent becomes talkative.

In order to pass on to dryer material less abruptly, mention must be made of other pewter-ware which collectors used to classify as measures, though they were, in fact, used for a more functional purpose. 'Naturalia non sunt turpia', nature is nothing to be ashamed of. The rounded articles on Plate 5 which were mistaken for measures really served a more private use, as can be seen on the early 16th. century painting of a brothel scene (by the Master of the Prodigal Son). Here the contents of a similar vessel are poured from an upper window over the departing guest just stepping through the door below. These 'vases de nuit' are also seen on a painting of the interior of a 15th. century hospital, now in the Twenthe Museum.

The more slender measures shown on Plates 6 and 7 were in daily use. Most of these and the large one on Plate 8 are stamped with a gauge-mark. Evidently the public authorities checked their exact capacity.

Beakers were usually of the high tumbler type and were decorated with line-engraving or wriggled work by the pewterer himself. Plate 57 shows a large specimen which may have been used as a communion beaker.

During the 17th. century these conical beakers seem to have been exported in great numbers and were used in Scottish kirks.

The examples on Plate 19 are actually conical beakers with a handle and a lid added; the date of the tankard on the left is about 1500, and it certainly looks rather rustic compared with the Flemish and Hungarian tankards on Plate 30.

In Germany we find the peculiar 'Pechkrug' of 'Holzkrug' tankards. These were composed of vertical wooden sections lined with a layer of pitch, and decorated with inlaid pewter. The lid was opened by means of a globe-shaped thumbpiece. On some specimens the globe could be unscrewed and used as a nutmeg container. One of these can be seen on Plate 55, with a similar type in plaited reed. Another curiosity is the 'Nautilus' beaker, a shell form on a high foot (Plate 56); this model can also been found in silver.

Plate 57 shows a group of small beakers; the one on a foot is a French specimen, the Dutch beaker with its decoration in relief is rather rare. The diminutive beakers on Plate 58 were apparently used on board ship for measuring out the rum ration for the sailors. Plate 59 shows several other models. The German 'Willkomm' beakers have already been mentioned and on Plate 37 you will see two examples of the collossal vessels from which the menfolk quenched their thirst.

Pewter bottles were made in various shapes and sizes. In some collections 'pilgrim bottles' are found (see Plate 3). Thick walled and heavy, the flattened circular vessels have a foot, a neck and two small angular ears. Through these ears a rope or strap was looped thereby hanging the bottle onto the belt or the saddle.

The early types, such as the fine specimen in the collection of F. J. Philips of Eindhoven, have a foot shaped like a plough-share. Later models have been found in other countries such as Switzerland, where they were carried on pewter or iron chains. In Austria and Germany round and hexagonal flasks with a screw stopper were in common use; holding them by a pewter carrying ring the farmers took these along with them into the fields. They were often decorated with engravings or in relief, which was also a custom with the powder bottles of Plate 4.

On the same picture is a remarkable relief on a large Persian bottle, which clearly shows the influence of the decorative work of Nuremberg.

The 17th. century bottle on Plate 8 is of Dutch origin.

We have inherited a great number of dishes, plates and basins right up to the present day. As can be seen in many paintings the food was served on a large pewter charger, which was placed in the centre of the table with the smaller plates arranged round it. In the Rijksmuseum in Amsterdam hangs a 16th. century picture called *The Banquet of the Civic Guard* by Cornelis Anthonisz. Here we can see that the meat is set on the table on a large pewter dish and pewter platters are used as dinner plates. After the meal hands were washed in a deep basin which was sometimes passed round with an ewer of water (Plate 40).

The first pewter plates were designed after the style of their wooden predecessors which were either rectangular or round, with a narrow raised rim (Plate 42). The deep dish on Plate 41 has a similar rim.

Later on we find dishes of the ceramic style, with a distinctly separate well and rim (Plate 46). There are also the 'cardinal's hat' dishes; on Plate 45 you will see a large specimen arranged with some smaller ones, and a group of three others on Plate 48. These are more or less the shape of an upturned cardinal's hat. Some have a raised convex centre with a slightly curved rim on which is engraved a coat of arms. They are beautifully proportioned and great favourites with collectors. Most of these 'cardinal's hat' dishes were made in the 17th century, although broad rimmed dishes were already in use long before that time. They figure for instance in the above mentioned picture painted by Cornelis Anthonisz in 1533.

The large dishes seen in the print of a pewterers shop in the booklet *Spiegel van het Menselijk Bedrijf* (Reflections on the work of the Craftsmen), by Jan and Kasper Luyken in 1718, prove that pewterers continued to make this type for some considerable time.

The very large specimen on Plate 47 is an example of a dish which has been hammered out of a sheet of pewter. On the upper side the hammerwork itself is used as a form of decoration.

Hammering was also used occasionally for strengthening cast dishes. The use of relief ornamentation on dishes and plates of the 'Edelzinn' (Plates 51, 52, 53) will be discussed later.

Many dishes were ornamentally engraved by the caster or by an engraver. One example of this is the portrayal of the *Feast of the Passover* on Plate 54. Decorative engravings figure also on the pewter work shown on Plate 50. In the second half of the 17th century we find reeded mouldings round the edge of the rim, sometimes containing several grooves. In the 18th century the rim of the dish became narrower and often had a raised beading or lobes at the edge. Some we find with just the back of the rim showing a moulding. This profile served two purposes, it was decorative and gave extra strength to the rim. The tray and six plates (Plate 49) are examples of the style of Louis XIV. Gadrooned rims were added to the round, square, six-or eight sided plates, dishes and trays of that period. These wavy-edge profiles were either cast separately and soldered on, or cast in one piece with the plate.

Dishes on a high foot were used for butter and fruit as early as the 16th. century. The small pewter dishes on Plate 41 are of early date and may be regarded as fore-runners of the 'cardinal's hat' dishes. The marks on them are generally in Gothic minuscules.

As the centre of the dishes became gradually damaged by knife cuts, they were scraped in the same way as the wooden trenchers, until at last they had to be recast. If a specimen is found, particularly in a collection of 'Edelzinn', where the rim is getting loose, it is advisable to have it repaired by an expert.

Porringers of various sizes were necessary for soft foods. Plate 41 shows a large porringer; smaller ones with one and two ears are shown on Plate 42. A similar specimen can be seen on Jan Mostaert's painting (reproduced facing the title page). Plate 43 shows also 16th. and 17th. century porringers. The porringers with the two flat open work ears are sometimes called, in our damp countries, 'brandy porringers'. In Germany this type of porringer has a three footed lid which can be used as a plate or stand. There they are called 'Wochenschüssel'. In France 'écuelles de baptême', or 'écuelles d'accouchée'. The 'écuelles de bouillon', with their dainty relief work, were made particularly in Strasbourg and Lyons. Small bowls with one ear were used as wine tasters. Plate 44 shows a Frisian porringer with a foot and two ears, decorated with relief work and engraving.

In the course of the years, saltcellars have gone through a diversity of changes. The 15th. and 16th. century saltcellars (Plate 60) often have a lid with a domed centre, when it is opened this acts as a support for the heavy lid. The elevated protrusion is sometimes hollow, and open at the top, and can then be used as a salt shaker. Due to its close resemblance to a church pyxis, it is often confused with that, but its use as a saltcellar is quite evident by its place in numerous paintings, e.g. the picture, mentioned previously, by Jan Mostaert. Later the lid was sometimes replaced by a small linen cloth laid across three protruding fingers of the saltcellar.

Plate 61 shows two examples of about 1600; the saltcellar on the still-life on page I belongs to the 17th. century. The triangular specimens with the pierced work and relief on Plate 67 date from the end of that century, and Plate 68 shows an 18th. century saltcellar in the style of Louis XV. The saltcellar used to play an important role on the table. In England the 'Master salt' placed in front of the master of the house was large and impressive and the fellow-guests sat 'above or beneath the salt' according to their rank of importance.

V

VI

A late 16th. century mustard pot is shown on Plate 61, a Louis XIV specimen on Plate 62, a Louis XVI pepper pot on Plate 64, and Plate 67 shows an 18th. century box, made with separate compartments for the various condiments.

Louis XV sugar bowls are depicted on Plate 63, and a Louis XVI style on Plate 64. A rococo sugar bowl with a spoon rack is shown on Plate 68.

Plate 72 shows a group of spoons, the one with the curved handle dates from the 15th. century, the others are the current style of the 17th. century. It is thought that the spoons and rack on Plate 97 are 18th. century toys.

As there was such a large variety of spoons, they are of popular interest for special collections, particularly in England. The bowl of the spoon was made in three main forms, olive shaped, round, and later oval. The stem of the spoon is often tapered right under the bowl to strengthen the construction. The top of the handle has many variations, an acorn, seal, crown, deer's foot, small figures or apostles. The latter heading has often been imitated. The 'apostle' spoons were given as a present at a christening, the particular apostle chosen being the name-saint of the child who was baptized. Many of the old spoons disappeared as a result of the recasting done by the travelling pewterers. The early spoons were beaten, but later this hammering was omitted. The spoon-makers were held in low esteem because of their repeated tampering with the alloy. A study of base metal spoons has been published by F. F. G. Hilton Price. Some spoons have a mark in relief, which shows that the pewterer must have cut it in the mould. Spoons with a pierced bowl were used as sugar-casters. Forks came into use at a much later date. Formerly even kings and emperors ate with their fingers. Being such a soft material it was not suitable to make forks from pewter, and for that reason there are very few in existence. For the same reason knives with pewter handles, decorated with pierced work or handsome engraving, are seldom seen.

Coffee-pots were the centre of many an 18th. century gathering, standing neatly on three legs they were always ready for the tap to be turned on, giving a full measure of their comforting contents to the guests, the chattering women, and the men silently smoking their long clay pipes. The pots generally stood on a shining copper brazier, their naked rotundity concealed under a modest dress of multicoloured paint. The Northern models were simple country-women compared with their alluring Southern sisters, who followed the fashion of the great French stylists.

In Germany the skirts of the 'spiral' tankards swung in the whirling Rococo wind. The water kettles on braziers ('bouilloirs'-Plate 74) are the big brothers in the tea and coffee pot family.

After this 'coffee-chat' we will quickly summarize the remaining pewter in the houshold, though the tea and dinner services have been rather extensive. Everyone knows the large open vegetable dishes and tureens of pewter for the use of the hearty eaters, the feeding cups for the invalids, the bottles and spouted beakers for the babies. The milk heaters with wooden handles, the butter coolers with a screw lid, the white lacquered cruet stands, and the gaily coloured chestnut vases. The pewterers themselves hired out drinking sets and dinner services on occasion.

On Plate 66 we find a small tureen with burin engraving and a large one with a spiral decoration is shown on Plate 63. The Louis XIV wine-cooler on Plate 69 is also a considerable size.

Mortars (Plate 71) were seldom made of pewter, inkstands were made in great numbers and in many varied forms (Plate 73 and 74). They usually have a drawer below to hold the letter wafers, and sand sprinklers. The pot itself was made of lead.

Tobacco boxes (Plate 65) were made in all styles of the 'Grand' Epoque', Louis XIV, square or hexagonal, 'Régence', oval, spiralled Louis XV, and round Louis XVI ones decorated with medallions.

A sheet of lead was put in to press the tobacco down in the box.

A great variety of boxes have been made, among them are some most curiously-shaped snuff boxes (Plate 99).

Pewter wash-basins were built in the side-boards, smaller drinking-fountains were hung at the side of the cabinets. Barbers' basins of pewter were in common use, and also blood cups for surgical bleeding.

Special craftsmen made pewter lids for earthenware mugs, and the clasps for beaded bags. Plate 103 shows pewter buttons and clasps from an early date.

A great many toys have been made of this metal (Plates 97—100); amongst others equipment for dolls houses, which help to give us an idea of the furnishings of contemporary homes. The ordinary utensils were accurately copied in miniature. As a rule the familiar tea sets are not very old and were made of an inferior alloy. But other toys are often of excellent quality and workmanship and sometimes of a very early date (Plates 101, 102). The Guildhall Museum has a collection of excavated toys. Finally, lamps were made of pewter through the ages. For chandeliers (Plate 76) and bracket candelsticks (Plate 83) pewter was too flexible to be practical, but oil lamps (Plate 81) were in every day use, in particular the type on Plate 84. So with the snuffer on that picture we now extinguish the lamps of this worldly show and in the next chapter light the candles in the candlesticks of church pewter.

PEWTER IN CHURCH AND CLOISTER

Simplex sigillum veri

I̶F THE PRECEDING CHAPTER on domestic pewter has been somewhat lengthy, we will now limit ourselves. If we have lingered in the tavern rather too long, the virtuous reader must not blame our weakness for mug and jug or underrate our appreciation of higher values.

After all the role of pewter was first a worldly one, and much of what we have written in this connection can also be applied to church pewter. Furthermore, it is obvious that objects for religious use were made of costlier metals whereever possible. It was the smaller, the poorer parishes who had to be content with a more modest material in their church, or who used pewter for ordinary services and brought out the precious metals on special days. The sacraments were never allowed to come in contact with pewter; thus, for instance, the cup of a pewter ciborium had always to be lined with a precious metal. The use of pewter for liturgical articles was temporarily forbidden in some countries, but due to a decrease in prosperity it was later readmitted. Then it was usually modelled on designs resembling church silver though of a less elaborate style.

For the sham magnificence which is a feature of many religious objects of our time was not manifest in these days, particularly not among the pewter work. 'Simplicity is the sign of real worth'. In the Gothic period especially, and in that of the early Renaissance, a purity of taste seems to have been a common quality of the craftsmen, which enabled them to create the right proportions by intuition. They achieved a natural beauty free from artistic pretensions, yet showing a touch of their individual personality. In the tumult of our time this prevailing good taste has been lost, and pride in one's craft has been stifled by the continuous rush of life.

Pewter was used for a shorter period in Catholic churches than in those of the Reformed belief, where pewter communion beakers are still occasionally found. It has practically disappeared

33

from the churches now, and it is regrettable that these ecclesiastical properties have been allowed to come onto the common market.

The oldest religious pewter objects have been discovered in the graves of the clergy, just as the sword was buried with the soldier. They consist mostly of patens and chalices, very small, but well proportioned. Plate 90 and the last reproductions in this book illustrate a few examples. It is true to say that very little remains from the early centuries, but G. Bapst is too definite in his statement, when talking about liturgical pewter of the 14th. and 15th. century, 'aucun des divers objets religieux n'a survecu'. There are several candlesticks of this period, and the pyxis and the holy water bowl on Plate 95 are also of 15th. century origin.

Candlesticks were set on the Altar and in other parts of the church. On Plate III you will see a pair of large 16th. century church candlesticks, probably of German make. The candlesticks on Plate 78 are from the beginning of the 16th. century and those on Plate 79 are late 16th. century. The 14th. century example on Plate 77 is rather extraordinary, as the iron point on which the candle is pricked is fixed right on the bottom of the shaft, not on the grease tray.

The shape of the shaft usually gives a clue to the period in which the candlestick was made. It was originally quite straight, like that of the last mentioned specimen, later the line was broken by the introduction of a distinctly separate node, and still later several nodes were included, thereby making it easier to hold and carry the candlestick. Towards the end of the 16th. century these distinctive protuberances began to disappear, and in the 17th century the shafts developed into a baluster-shape, with a collar sometimes breaking the line (Plates 80 and 81).

Then, in the 18th. century, they were made in the typical Louis styles (Plate 82). The well balanced construction of Louis XIV, the frivolous upward spirals of Louis XV, and the severe stately columns of the Louis XVI. The material was not firm enough for the many-armed candelabra and the bracketed candlesticks (Plate 83), therefore they are very rare indeed.

There are also very few church lamps, but I must mention the holy lamp suspended on three chains in which a light is kept burning. A relic of Jewish rites is the Sabbath lamp (Plate 85), star-shaped with a grease tray below. The Maccabean or Chanoeka lamp (Plate 86), which has eight oil lamps in a row, and a separate little lamp to light them from, is another. In December those of Jewish faith celebrate 'Chanoeka' in remembrance of the victory of Judas Maccabeus over the armies of Greece and Syria, and the reconsecration of the temple in Jerusalem. The custom is to light one oil lamp on each of eight consecutive nights, thereby ultimately illuminating the whole Chanoeka lamp. The seven spouts on the Sabbath lamp represent the seven days of the week.

Chalices (Plate 89) are among the most important objects in a religious service. Great numbers of them still remain, perhaps because they were part of a sacred act, they were handled with more reverence and care. The chalice was in fact used for several purposes; as a chalice proper during the mass (calix sanctus), for passing round (calix communicalis), and for offerings (calix offertorius). The cup or upper part contained wine, to which a few drops of water could be added with a little spoon. Over the cup lay a linen cloth (Palla), with a piece of stiff card slipped between the folds.

Some of the early specimens were beautifully proportioned, but later the cup was occasionally made too large in comparison with the stem. The different periods can be easily distinguished by the node halfway up the stem, which, as with the candlesticks, originally stood out clearly from it, but later became baluster-shaped.

The paten (Plate 89) which was used with the chalice was a small, simple plate-shape. The later models were somewhat larger and occasionally had a foot. It was used for the consecrated bread. Larger specimens were used for collecting offerings. The English 'Alms Dishes' frequently have an umbo, sometimes decorated with enamelled work.

The ciborium (Plate 88) is the same shape as a chalice but has a lid bearing a crucifix. It contains the consecrated bread and as the calix communicalis, is used for passing round to the communicants. The cylindrical host-box or pyx (Plate 95) was used for storing the consecrated bread.

The hexagonal pyx appeared in the 15th. century also. The

objects on Plate 60 are often called pyx mistakenly, for they are nearly all salts, only now and again do we see an inscription which indicates that the box was meant for religious use.

There is a great variety of styles among the Mass and Communion flagons (Plate 39). The two small jugs, called ampullae, on Plate 29, are inscribed with the letters A and V respectively, indicating that one contained water (aqua) and the other wine (vinum). The vessels containing the consecrated oil were also ampullae, as were the small vase-shaped objects on Plate 103, in which pilgrims carried home relics, bones, or consecrated earth, collected on their journeys. The last mentioned ampullae have a high lead content. A great number which were found on the bed of the river Seine can be seen in the Musée de Cluny. Many are decorated with fleur de lys. What adventures have these small mysterious objects witnessed, what privations of the pious monk on his weary pilgrimage, what joys on his return to the flower-scented monastery garden?

Ewers without lids (Plate 40) were used in church as well as in the home for washing hands, and it is only natural that there should be a matching basin. The same sort of model was used for baptisms. Adolphe Riff has written a monograph on 'aiguières en casque'. These ewers which were often examples of 'orfèvrerie d'étain' are shaped like an inverted helmet, especially the later specimens which have an S-shaped rim. The earlier types have a straight top, and there is a beak or spout for pouring out the water. The real baptismal fonts were much bigger, and have also been made of pewter. They can still be found in parts of old Bohemia, made in the shape of an upturned bell, supported on three feet. There was yet another kind of lavabo used in the churches. This consisted of a deep bowl with two spouts, and was hung on a turning iron hinge in a special niche. As compared with the many surviving bronze specimens, these objects are extremely rare in pewter. On the 'Mérode Altar' by the master of Flémalle we can see one being used.

Vases for flowers on the altar or elsewhere (Plate 93) closely resemble those found in pictures of interiors.

Incense boats (navicula) for holding incense were also made of pewter. It stands to reason that this metal was not used for the incense burners.

Small Holy-water stoups, the hanging type (Plate 94) and standing (Plate 95), have been in use in churches and dwellings throughout the ages.

Basins for Holy-water were hung on a hinged handle, an example can be seen with a sprinkler of the same metal on Plate 88.

Oil containers (chrismatoria) consisted of one vessel, or of two or three vessels joined together (Plate 91), or they were placed together in a box-like holder (Plate 92). The vessels were used for baptism (oleum sanctum), confirmation (oleum chrisma) and extreme unction (oleum infirmorum). Inside the lid, inscribed with the letters S, C and I, were three anointing sticks. The oleum sanctum was also used for the ordaining of priests, the oleum chrisma for bishops, and the oleum infirmorum for the consecration of church bells.

For Monstrances (Ostensoria) humble pewter was hardly considered.

Small reliquaries for household use, on the other hand, were made as late as the 19th. century. Only few specimens of the much older relic boxes still exist; they were made of wood, richly ornamented with inlaid or applied pewter.

Pewter was seldom used for altar crucifixes, but many small crosses were found in dwellings, some made of wood with pewter decorative work.

Religious statues (Plate 107) made of pewter with a high lead content were often present in the home.

Pilgrims badges of the 14th. and 15th. centuries (Plate 105) have been found in great numbers on river beds. The pilgrims received these as a token of a pilgrimage completed, and wore them sewn into their clothes, or hanging round their necks. They can be seen in the Musée de Cluny in Paris, or in the Germanisches Museum in Nuremberg. In the Musée de Cluny there are many other small objects, bells, whistles, toys, corporation badges, beggers' badges; insignia of the Hundred Years War; all of which have been described by G. Bapst in his study of early pewter.

These pilgrimages were not only made for religious purposes but also as a sentence of banishment by the church authorities or the secular arm. Obviously the returning pilgrim was forbidden to sell the symbols of his journey, and to prevent this, he was compelled to throw them into the water. This explains why so many of them have been found in the Seine and the Scheldt.

An extensive work on the countless pilgrims badges dredged up has been written by A. Forgeais in approximately 1860 ('Plombs Historiés trouvés dans la Seine'). In the Memorial Volume of the Frans Claes Museum, Jos de Beer wrote a monograph on 'Pilgrims' Badges' found in Belgium. In this he tells us that, the punishment for slander, for instance, was a long penitential pilgrimage. The medieval judges appeared to be extremely severe on the subject of malicious gossip by evil tongues and, in general, on all such trivial offences. We read of persons being sent on far distant pilgrimages for using expressions such as: I'll twitch that long nose of yours, you ugly black cat etc. Very common invectives which could be heard daily in populous quarters from vixen in a brawl.

In later days a victim could buy himself off such a punishment. The same writer tells us that the wearing of a pilgrims' badge was sufficient to obtain free hospitality when passing through villages and towns, and that special lodging-houses were established for that purpose. The pilgrims travelled in large groups, and many places owed their prosperity to this curious form of tourist traffic; the building of churches and monasteries also benefited from it.

Various saints are portrayed on the badges, and quite often the Madonna with the Infant Jesus. The stall of Bethlehem on Plate 105 is particularly beautiful. Other objects connected with these pilgrimages are found on Plates 103, 104 and 106. The whistles which announced the arrival of the pilgrims outside a town, bells, the pewter ampullae for carrying the relics, crucifixes etc.

Found with them were the miniature utensils shown on Plate 101 and 102, which have been mentioned earlier. As products of Medieval culture, these small objects have great value. The remains of the pilgrimages tell us of crime and punishment, of devotion and sacrifice, in days long past.

The pilgrims badges were generally cast in moulds of slate, in contrast to the ordinary pewter which was practically always cast in bronze moulds.

PEWTERERS AND THEIR GUILDS

Experientia optima rerum magistra

As THE CENTURIES PASS by, so the old methods of work become out-moded and make way for more modern techniques. When we see the bright daylight shining on the pewterer on Plate V, it seems as if the old tools in the shadow at the back of the workshop lie forgotten under a layer of dust. Yet in reality the technique has changed little during the years.

The old pewterers and their guilds have gone, as have nearly all the workshops. A very few kept going well into the 20th. century, but Meeuws and Son of the Hague are still plying the old trade up to the present day, and the ancient traditions of hand-work are still held in esteem. They have saved their own antique bronze moulds, and have also bought up those from some of the workshops which had to close down. In this fine equipment pewter-ware is still being cast.

These bronze moulds have always been the basis and pride of every foundry, and the accuracy and workmanship of such very heavy pieces fill us with wonder and surprise, the more so when we consider the primitive tools used to make them. Should two sections of the mould not fit precisely, then the liquid pewter would flow away between them.

The following information was given to me by a member of the above mentioned firm, who described the making of the bronze moulds.

The pewterer first makes a model out of a sheet of tin, over this he spreads a layer of plaster-of-Paris, which is then used as the shape for the bronze mould. To ensure that the separate sections of the mould fit closely, matching pegs and holes are made. In order to cast the pewter to the required thickness, the mould has to be turned on a lathe, thereby obtaining an equal distance between the core and the jacket throughout the whole of the rounded object. The moulds for other shapes must be hacked in the bronze and smoothed by hand, work which required a great deal of skill. Because of their costliness the large moulds were often owned collectively by several workshops or guilds.

The pewter was melted in an iron oven built in a brick furnace, but for small quantities an iron melting pan was used.

In order to produce a casting, the inside of the bronze mould was covered with a protective layer of some kind, usually a chalk preparation, before the pewter was poured into it. The mould had also to be sufficiently pre-heated, and the melted pewter had to be of just the right temperature.

In the making of the German 'Heissgusz' pewter-ware, the moulds were heated to a high temperature, and directly after the casting they were rapidly cooled off, thereby producing a thin, hard, shining metal. During the casting, the large moulds were fixed on the casting-bench. After the casting was finished the mould was taken apart, the pewter casting taken out, and the superfluous projections, ridges and other rough patches were removed. The better the workmanship of the mould, the less labour was required to finish off the cast piece.

The round castings were next turned on the lathe and finished with the chisels. The old lathe chisels had long handles. Then the separate sections of the piece were joined together by the use of a blow-pipe or a soldering-iron. The resulting joint was later finished off on the lathe. The speed of the lathe was controlled by a wheel-turner under the command of the master; it was far less than that of the modern lathe. The grooves made by the chisel were therefore quite different, and they form one of the distinguishing features of antique pewter. The pieces which were not round, were smoothed with a scraper, a file, a burnishing-stone or agate.

The remaining components of the objects were then attached. In olden times they were cast on. For instance, a mould in the shape of a handle was pressed against the trunk of the tankard. Melted pewter was poured into the mould, and this penetrated the holes previously made in the tankard where the handle was to join the trunk. Inside the tankard the over-flow of pewter was stopped by putting a piece of moist cloth against the hole, or by filling the tankard with sawdust; the impressions of which are still clearly distinguishable on many old flagons. Sometimes an alloy with a lower content was allowed for the handles. Traces of the scraper are often still visible on the handles of antique tankards.

In the work of the Benedictine monk Theophiles, 'Schedula diversarum artium', written about the year 1100, mention is made of the casting, turning, soldering, filing and polishing of pewter flagons.

The casting was done occasionally in iron, gypsum, sand or stone. Discarded objects were handed in to the pewterer, who by local law was sometimes prohibited to strike his touch-mark on the re-cast pewter. Another regulation stated that recasting must take place in the presence of the owner, to gua-rantee the return of the object in metal of the same alloy.

The technique of making a hollow casting, such as a spout, is rather curious. The melted pewter is poured into a cold mould, and then quickly poured or flung out. The still liquid core se-parates and leaves the solidified outside wall, which remains as a hollow object. All these processes required great proficiency and the saying 'experience is the best teacher' applied also to this craft.

Sometimes when making big plates or dishes, a sheet of pewter was cast and flattened, and the desired shape obtained by forging with a hammer. This method strengthened the pewter, which was then called 'sad-ware', in contrast with 'hollow-ware'. Because of the superiority of this process the casting of some particular objects was forbidden. The hammer used had a short handle, slanting sides, and the surface had to be smooth, like that of an anvil. The hammer markings can often be seen on the back of a piece, and they were also used occasionally to brighten up the right side, a simple and effective method of decoration.

The composition of the alloy used for casting has an im-portant effect upon the durability of pewter-ware. Usually the tin was mixed with other metals. Objects made from tin-alloy are called 'pewter', and the pure metal is called 'tin' in English, but in other languages this distinction is not made, both are called 'tin', from the Latin word 'stannum'. 'Kaiserzinn' and 'Brittania' metal are different mixtures, while 'Plate' contains no tin, but is silver-plated copper. Tin-plate is sheet-iron coated with a thin layer of tin. Bronze is an alloy of tin and copper, and objects made of this metal were in use earlier than pewter.

Pure tin is seldom met with in the mines, it is usually found combined with other substances, such as arsenic, copper or iron, in fairly regular shaped crystals. The greater part is obtained from tin-ore or tin-stone (SnO_2) which is called cassiterite (after the old Greek word κασσιτερος). It is found in only a few places, among them Indonesia, Malaya, China, the Belgian Congo and Bolivia. In China it was discovered and used thousands of years before our era. It is mined in Europe in Cornwall, Bohemia, and Spain, from where it was fetched by the Phoenicians.

The concession for exploiting the mines in Billiton was granted more than a hundred years ago, and in 1860 the Billiton Company was founded. This undertaking now owns a number of super dredging-machines, each of which brings three million cubic metres of earth to the surface a year. These huge installations enable the Billiton Company to supply the large demands for tin in modern industry. The ore is no longer smelted on the islands, but in the installations of the Netherlands Metallurgical Works at Arnhem. The most important uses for tin at the present time are the manufacture of tin-plate, solder, babbit metal and bronze. Both copper and iron are coated with tin to prevent oxidation, and much earthen-ware is covered with opaque tin-glaze rendering it impervious to moisture.

As I have already mentioned, pewter objects are seldom made of pure tin, as this is too soft and does not flow smoothly into the mould. Mixed with a small amount of lead it is harder (this is called 'Fine pewter'), other metals such as antimonium, copper and bismuth are also often added. A higher lead content lowers the quality of the pewter, making it soft and colourless, while the addition of antimonium makes the pewter darker and harder.

An excessive proportion of lead, which was cheaper than tin, often occurred in Continental pewter-ware. This was a danger to the health of the people, and spoilt the reputation of the craft. The pewterers therefore frequently petitioned the public authorities to make laws for the protection of their craft against these malpractices, which were apt to recur. 'Come boy', the master would say, 'Get the lead ready, we are going to cast pewter spoons'. In his *Zinn, Geologisch-Montanistisch-Historische Monografie,* Reyer quotes Mathesius, saying 'Weil die Geschirre oft zu viel Blei haben nennen the Bergleute die Zinnkannen Bleisäcke. Die breiten Kännlein heissen sie Hämmer, dieweil sie oft einander damit vor die Köpfe schlagen.' (The tankards often contained such a high lead content that, being so heavy, the miners called them 'lead-bags'. The wide tankards they called hammers and, when necessary, used them as such on each other heads). In his publication *Het oude Tingieters Bedrijf in Friesland* (The trade of the old pewterers in Friesia), Dr. Wassenberg describes the amount of swindling which had to be dealt with in that province. He also states that the Friesian pewter had such a bad reputation, 'that the Pewterers and Pewter sellers in Holland were so disgusted with it, that they no longer wished to receive or exchange any pewterware from Friesia'. The Friesians insisted upon the appointment of overseers, who would check and punish the defaulters. These abuses had been dealt with in the rest of Holland some time earlier.

The prescribed proportion of tin to lead varied according to the time the rules were made, and the place where they were enforced. 'Fine Pewter', originally the term for pure pewter, contained about 10% lead and a poorer alloy about 20% lead. The old Roman pewter seems to have contained 25% lead, and very poor quality pewter, such as that used for inferior toys, contained up to 40% lead.

A richer mixture was preferred for making rectangular and flat objects, than for round ones.

English pewter often contains copper and antimonium instead of lead; it gives a clear echo, and when bent it produces a peculiar crackling sound, like that heard when pure pewter is bent as it is held very close to the ear. In France this sound is called 'le cri de l'étain'.

The name 'edelzinn' (noble pewter) has nothing to do with the composition of the alloy, it is just richly decorated pewterware. Alloys giving an exceptionally bright lustre were indeed used, and the inside of the lid of a tankard made of this

'Silberzinn' alloy, which contains no lead, is still a light silvery colour, making us think it is a newly made piece. It is not true to say that this colour is obtained by the addition of silver to the alloy, though there were some pewterers who strived to give their products an appearance of silver (Sebaldus Ruprecht) or gold (Melchior Koch). The metal they made produces a faint rustling noise when slightly bent.

In order to test the mixture, a drop was removed from the object by a soldering-bolt, and the colour of the scooped out part was checked; this should be clear and shiny on fine-pewter. A more accurate method was to compare the weight of a small disc taken from the piece to be tested, with a similar sized disc made of the desired alloy.

If an article contains more than 25% lead, the metal will make a black line when drawn across a piece of paper, and is easily scratched with the point of a knife. The weight, the colour of the surface, and the sound it makes when tapped with something hard, all indicate the quality of the alloy.

The great variety of alloys used for various specimens explains one reason for the many colour-tones which are a feature of old pewter. Even the surface of a single object may show many nuances of colour. These may be due to the fact that during the cooling the alloy does not remain uniform throughout the casting, hence the irregular oxidation or corrosion on the surface, which imparts to the antique pewter a 'living' appearance, never acquired to such an extent by other metals.

The guilds exerted a great influence on the quality and finish of pewter-ware. These were unions of artisans and craftsmen in the same or similar crafts. In the Middle Ages, and long after, they played an important part in the social structure of the people. On the Continent they came into being as early as 1400, originally as a kind of religious fraternity, but later as guilds of a craft. The crafts had previously been practised by monks.

The pewterers were initially associated with other trades in common guilds. As they generally sold their products themselves, or had a shop, they were sometimes affiliated with a merchants' or marketing guild, or with a guild which more or less resembled their own craft, such as the smith's trade.

Eventually they were able to form a guild of their own, as for instance in the year 1651 there was 'A Charter given to the Pewterers and Spoonmakers by the council of Leyden.' In his paper about the Amsterdam pewterers guild, W. F. H. Oldewelt assumes that the pewterers of that town formed an independant guild about the end of the 16th. century, while W. G. D. Murray has published information about the guild of the 'Rotterdam pewterers'. In 1348 the London pewterers' Guild petitioned for ordinances regarding the protection of their craft.

Besides the alloy and the workmanship of the product, the guild supervised the prices, competition, wages ,working hours and other interests of the craft, and even the personal behaviour of the members. The guilds had their own capital, laws and seals. Even when they had become purely trade-crafts they remained closely allied to the church, among other things they expressed this tie by giving presents, such as lamps, candlesticks and chandeliers. At the head were the Master of the Company and Wardens, who were often appointed by the town authorities. They had to settle disputes, for example between the masters, journeymen and apprentices. There was also a difference in rank between the masters; the junior master had to carry out special services, such as taking messages, collecting money etc. When admitted as a master, he had to entertain his colleagues to a feast, and ensure that the guild flagons were filled. In the time of decline in this craft, a kind of family government developed, only the son or son-in-law of a master was able to become a master himself. But even without this compulsion the business was usually passed on to the sons, and thus the costly bronze moulds remained in the possession of the same family for many generations.

Regulations were made concerning the internal relations of each guild, the engagement of the apprentices, their treatment and dismissal, the rights and obligations of masters, journeymen and apprentices.

The period of apprenticeship lasted about three years, and during this time the apprentice usually lodged with the master. In some parts of the country there was a rule that the jouneyman should work for some considerable time before he could become a master, and if he was unable to pay a certain sum of money into the guild fund, then he would have to remain a journeyman. These men went on long journeys, which explains why certain techniques or forms were transferred from one district to another. In German taverns the emblem of the craft was hung over the tables enabling the travelling journeyman to find his work-mates easily. In order to be admitted as a master, the aspirant had to submit his apprentice papers and a birth certificate. But most important of all was the proof of his ability. The prospective master had to produce a proof piece, made with his own tools within a set time, sometimes even having to make his own mould first. In some guilds this work had to be carried out in the presence of the inspector. In England the apprentice could thereupon be sworn in as a Freeman of the Company and after a few years he was awarded 'livery'.

Originally, the town authorities supervised the quality of the products of the different crafts; but later the Wardens of the guilds took over this responsibility. In some places there was a law that these overseers of the guild or a representative of the town council must be present during the assay. The Wardens visited the workshops of the pewterers. They had the right of search and after checking the specimens there, they were entitled to impose fines, or remove objects as a forfeit.

The system I shall describe presently, whereby the caster was compelled to strike his wares with the 'touch-mark' of his workshop, made it possible to trace the maker of any product found which did not comply with the local regulations. There is no doubt that these regulations, binding the pewterer to the use of standard qualities of alloy, special methods, and the marking of his pewter-ware, have not only been of benefit to the buyer, but also to the craft.

Great differences existed between the regulations of one town and another. Great also was their influence, in general, upon the actual craftsmanship. But, undoubtedly, greater than the influence of these rules and regulations was the deep respect of the artisan for the material he handled, his undeniable notion of quality, his love of good sound work, and his feeling for 'style'.

By the use here of the word style, we do not mean it in the sense in which it is used by art-historians, not as a style with a particular name. Not the line and decoration featured in a certain period by a particular fashion, often dictated, more or less, according to the taste of some ostentatious potentate; not the style therefore, typifying an historical period. Of course such styles are important in the study of the history of art, and as a help in dating a particular article, a method used repeatedly in this book. It is also certain that the imitation of such historical styles often results in failures. However much beauty the Renaissance may have brought (though sometimes only partly understood in the northern countries), it was also guilty of an over-burdening by Grecian-Roman motifs. Books dealing with classical decoration were used in all countries. These decorative motifs were combined and whole surfaces completely covered with them. The results were clever and highly skilful, but often a meaningless, uninspired pattern of lines. The 19th. century has excelled itself in repetition, variation and exaggeration of all kinds of old styles and composities. Even during our time furniture in 'old finish' is still being mass-produced in quasi-Gothic style.

Even apart from these excesses, it must be admitted that the development of a sound and natural feeling for line and form is cramped, not only by imitating a past style, but also by slavishly following the accepted fashion of the present time.

We did not therefore mean to allude to the official well-known meaning of style, a fashion which appears rather suddenly, and then just as quickly disappears. We meant another kind, not dictated by fashion, but one which has developed within the craftsmen and the craft. Not created to satisfy the whims of a monarch or his courtiers, but brought about by the common need and the nature of the material.

In his book *Deutsches Handwerksgut*, Professor Dexel explains that this kind of style is not limited to a certain period; rather, that the form and the type of decoration produced by the people, mostly as a whole, are not invented by sudden inspirations, but gradually evolve with natural growth. These styles, which are always simple and practical, change slowly through the years, and due to their simplicity, the resulting products have more nuance and sensitivity than those which follow the old, or new, set style of fashion.

In parts where the artisans were not over-influenced by the current modes of their country or other lands, we find this innate feeling for line and form being transferred from one generation to another. The decorative work, if any, seemed to originate naturally from the form itself, it was unaffected, and without any forced desire for originality, a characteristic which so often led to foolish exaggerations.

This is why these simple utensils are of such importance, and I thought it only fair to represent them beside those of the familiar styles of the period, for they occupied a high place in the craft of the pewterer. More can be read about this subject in *Oude Ambachtskunst* (Art in old Crafts), by J. G. N. Renaud.

It is quite wrong to reject these well-tried shapes as old-fashioned. The best craftsmen always respected the standards handed down from generation to generation, and they certainly did themselves no harm by developing, not copying, earlier achievements. It is often not the more striking or luxurious, but the most simple object which is the hardest to produce. This demands intuition and self-discipline, and moreover, regard for certain proportions, shapes, golden rules, which should not be broken.

I believe that, in general, the pewterers have respected these in their work. Many examples of their industry, which we have inherited through the centuries, tell us this clearly. It is also beyond doubt that the guilds have promoted and perpetuated good and healthy traditions by means of their regulations and their control concerning the system of 'touch-marks'.

MARKING AND FINISHING

Finis coronat opus

$\mathbb{E}$VEN THE COLLECTOR WHO has turned grey in his love for pewter begins to falter when he contemplates the baffling host of pewter touch-marks. It is a confusing and chaotic scene, full of pitfalls and dangers. Although investigations among the archives have yielded results, a closer study has often led to a reconsideration or complete even withdrawal of the conclusions already reached.

Dr. A. Wassenbergh has written about the pewterers marks in Friesland, in his previously mentioned publication; which is, so far, the only time the marks of a province of the Netherlands have been dealt with. W. G. D. Murray has described the marks of the Rotterdam pewterers, and J. G. N. Renaud published a paper on this subject in the 1944 volume of the *Oudheidkundig Jaarboek* (The Archeological Yearbook).

Mr Oldenwelt's statement about the records of the Amsterdam pewterers typifies the difficulties met with in this particular form of research; he says 'Unfortunately their seal book, as it was popularly called, together with the archives of the guild, disappeared, leaving no trace of this important source of information about the craft. This is a loss to us, as from it we could have discovered the marks and names of the pewterers'.

Unfortunately, this 'unfortunate' state of affairs applies to many places in the Netherlands. Records are gone, and of the touch-plates upon which the pewterers had to strike their marks only that of Haarlem has survived. Search among the archives of the town and guild, for any traces, takes a great deal of time, and for the reason already stated, no study will ever give us a complete picture. The hope, cherished by some, that a standard work on this subject would appear in the near future, cannot be shared by us, and in this book we shall confine ourselves to a short description of the different types and systems which existed in the Low Countries.

The method of marking pewter differed from that usually applied to silver, for in contrast with the silversmith, it was the pewterers themselves who struck their *master-touch*, on the products of their workshops. Each had his own mark, and was compelled (in England for the first time in 1503) to stamp it, not only on every article that left the workshop, but also on the touch-plates kept by the public authorities. In London the touch plates were kept at the Hall of the Company. This meant that there was a complete record of all the marks of the workshops, thereby making it possible to trace the maker of each pewter object bearing a mark. It is a great pity that, with the exception of the one in the Frans Hals Museum in Haarlem, all the metal touch plates in Holland have been lost, as without them it is not possible to identify the pewterer, or so easy to date the piece. The five still existing touch plates of London craftsmen are in the possession of the Worshipful Company of Pewterers. This particular system of control has now died out, for, as the strength of the guilds decreased, so the respect for such regulations declined.

So long as there were decrees in force there were pewterers who tried to evade them; for instance when their products were made of too low an alloy, they omitted the mark. As a result of this practice, or because of imperfectly struck or worn-out stamps, or due to the loss of the touch plates and civic records, it is often impossible to discover the name of the maker of a certain piece. Moreover, church pewter was seldom marked, and it was of course easy for the travelling pewterer to dodge the written laws if he wished. Consequently in such cases the only means left for dating a piece is to judge it by its style; but the disadvantage of this method is the fact that the casting was done from the same bronze moulds often for many years.

Generally speaking, not to much importance should be attached to the presence, or not, of a mark, in judging the quality or authenticity of a piece.

As has been mentioned earlier, spoons sometimes bear the marks in relief, showing that the marks must have been cut in the mould. This also applies to 'Edelzinn' upon which the separate marks of the mould engraver and the pewterer can occasionally be found.

Although this mark is generally called the master or makers-mark, since the pewterer himself struck it on his wares, it is in most cases also a *quality mark*. On early specimens we do see now and again the master and the quality mark separately, but later the two marks were combined, one part indicating the quality with a special emblem, such as an Angel or a Rose etc., and the other part bearing the name or initials of the maker. A full name on the piece shows that it is of later date, as up to the middle of the 18th. century the pewterer as a rule added only his initials to the quality mark.

The quality of the alloy was often indicated by the same emblem in different countries, but the actual value given to that emblem differed according to the period and the place.

The 'Crown', together with the initials of the pewterer, is one of the oldest marks of good quality, but later appeared only in combination with other signs.

The 'Rose', generally with a crown, also indicated the best quality originally, but was later used as a mark on medium quality. This mark, which probably originated from the Tudor-Rose, appeared in the Low Countries as early as the 16th. century. In the 17th. century it was much larger, and was also seen in combination with the 'Angel' mark, possibly signifying an alloy of medium quality.

The 'Hammer', usually found with a crown, is a much used and early mark for Fine Pewter. The theory that it was used on hammer-work only is disproved by the many cast objects found bearing this mark.

The 'Angel' is a mark on Fine Pewter of a later date, sometimes with no lead content, but always of good quality. It is a mark, therefore, which is frequently given the doubtful honour of being stamped on fakes. Should the word 'English Pewter' be found in old regulations or on pewter objects, it does not always mean that the pewter in question is of English origin, but that the alloy is made according to the English recipe, which results in good quality pewter, often marked with an Angel. Similarly the mark 'London' does not always mean that the object has been made in that city; it was often used outside London and even outside England, to indicate a lead-free pewter of first quality. In France 'F' or 'FF' meant fine pewter, and 'C' a lower alloy, in Germany we find 'Feinzinn' and 'Probezinn' and in Holland 'Fijn tin' and 'Keur tin'.

The 'Four small shields' mark was also called the 'imitation silver' mark. Originally it may have been intended to deceive people into thinking that the object was made of silver, or an alloy with a high silver content. It gradually became a common mark for good quality, usually combined with an 'X' and a crown.

A date in the mark tells us the year in which the master was established as a pewterer, and occasionally it indicated the year in which a regulation, concerning the quality mark, was enforced.

There are differing opinions about the municipal coat of arms which often occurs together with the master and quality mark. The pewterer was sometimes compelled to add this to his wares. It was thought to be, originally, a civic guarantee of the capacity of a flagon, but more generally it seems to have been intended as a sort of warrant, to show that the work bore the correct quality mark. In the course of time a town often changed its coat of arms, and the pewterer sometimes altered his touch marks. Although the regulations concerning the marks were occasionally passed on from one town to another, there were still differences, so that the same mark does not always indicate the same type of alloy.

A good way to obtain a copy of the marks is to rub them off with a hard pencil on a piece of thin but strong paper, or with the top of a penholder on smooth tinfoil.

Mention should also be made of the owners initials, which are found on dishes and tankards particularly. On early pieces these 'house-marks' and Teutonic symbols tell us to which member of the cloister, or regular customer in the tavern, the piece belonged. The monogram of Christ, $\chi \varrho$, Chr, is found on rare occasions also.

Finally we must call attention to the gauges or capacity seals, stamped on pewter measures and flagons. They are also found on the tankards with the pegs inside indicating their capacity, which was occasionally checked by the gauger.

We have dealt with the pewterers marks at some length after all, and as we have already mentioned, the unmarked pewter

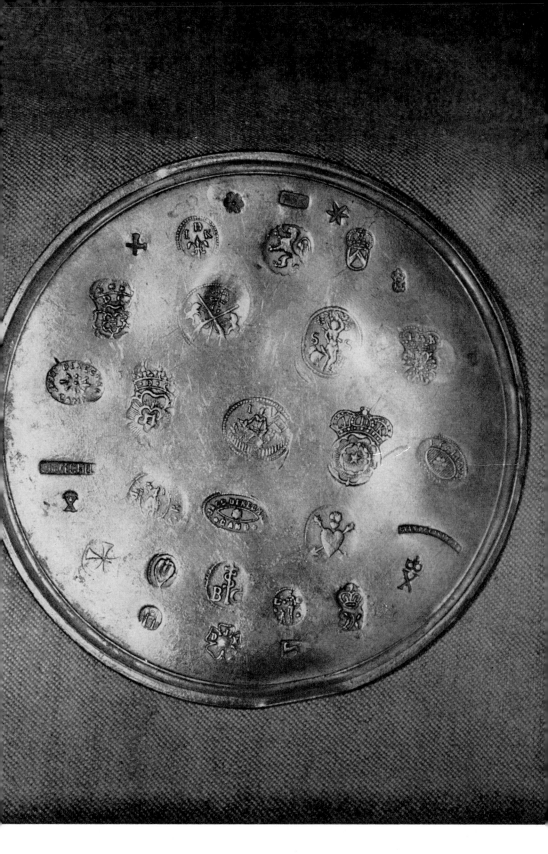

VII

De TINNEGIETER.

Zoekt in u zelfs den schat, Van 't allerschoonste vat.

VIII

is also worthy of note, this being yet another facet of our metal. So after meeting the assayer and the gauger we will now return to the pewterer.

Various methods were used by the pewterer to beautify his product, 'the finish is the reward of labour', but one is inclined to wonder if his efforts were always successful. With other metals such as copper, brass, bronze and iron, the plain surface was usually left untouched. Why is it then, that the sensitive skin of pewter had to take so much tattooing? However much we may admire the exquisitely painted porcelains of later Chinese dynasties, were the early monochromes of that land any less beautiful?

It was the pewterer himself who generally carried out the decorative work, and although we may consider that, even with all the evidence of his good taste, he did rather carry this to excess at times, we will not refrain from describing briefly the following methods of decorating pewter-ware.

First we will mention decoration in relief, found on the products of the remarkable 'Edelzinn' technique. Here the object was not decorated after the casting, but the bronze mould, in which the casting was to be done, was cut out to the desired pattern by the engraver or etcher. In contrast with the German 'Edelzinn' which was made in plenty, this technique has seldom been used in England or the Low Countries. Grandmasters of this art who produced truly beautiful results were the French engraver François Briot, Casper Enderlein and Jacob Koch II of Germany, and several others. Though they did the casting sometimes themselves, these masters were renowned more as engravers than casters, for their art was expressed in the first place in engraving the decoration with a burin in the mould. Before this time Nicolaus Horchheimer, among others, had cast specimens in moulds in which extremely fine decoration had been, not engraved, but etched, the result being decorative work in low-relief.

By the use of these methods, whole surfaces of dishes and flagons were covered with decorative work. In the centre of the dishes we usually find an umbo bearing an allegorical figure, with further representations on the flat surface surrounded by grotesques and arabesques. On the underside is a portrait medallion of the engraver.

The famous 'Plat et Aiguière de la Tempérance' were made by Briot about 1580. The Temperantiadish made by Enderlein has somewhat heavier decorative work. The smaller ornamental plates such as the Kaiser, Apostel, and Gustave Adolf Teller, were exported from Nuremberg and Saxony, and they were also used as a pattern for decorations in other countries. For example for the Balkan and Persian bottles on Plate 4. In Switzerland plates were made bearing the coat of arms of the cantons. In the Frederiks collection in the Hague there are many fine pieces of 'Edelzinn'. It was also made in Strasburg, among others by Isaac Faust, who also made the delightful 'écuèlles de bouillon' mentioned earlier. Specimens of 'Edelzinn' are pictured on Plates 35, 36, 51, 52, 53. The German screw-top bottles also occasionally show this type of decoration. English pieces having cast ornamentation (a few beakers, plates, porringers) have been described by the late H. H. Cotterell in *Antique Collector* July 1931 and by Cotterell and Vetter in *Apollo* 1933/1936.

Relief decorations, separately cast, were occasionally added to the cast specimen, in particular by the Saxon pewterers who used the well-known 'Flötner Plaketten'. In more western countries, relief work has not often been used as a predominating decoration (in England the famous William Granger candlestick, 1610), but just in simple mouldings, beading, medallions etc. Details such as thumb-rests, lids, hinges and taps were sometimes decorated in relief, with motifs of flora and fauna. Pierced casting or *ajour* work is found on the ears of porringers, on braziers and on many objects of a later period.

The chased work we sometimes see as relief ornamentation is nearly always a fake, set on later with the idea of increasing the market value of a piece. Generally speaking the material is too soft for this purpose. The metal is chased on the reverse side, so that the design appears in relief on the right side, or it is chased on the right side on a cushion of pitch. The straight or spiral lines of repoussé work are chased onto pewter-ware with a hammer and chisel; this type of decorative work is found on some German tankards. Silver chasing was imitated in pewter by casting in the mould.

In most countries, *engraving* was used as a method of decoration. Flowing lines were cut in the metal with a burin and the excess metal which formed a ridge on either side of the line could be removed afterwards. Parts of the engraved design were sometimes filled in with pricking and hatching. Handsome engraving can be seen on the German 'Kuchenplatten' on Plate 50. The engraved characters on guild flagons, or the Hebrew on the Sederplates give a decorative effect, but the script letters are generally less attractive. Engraving was used to put initials or names on the pewter objects, also to draw a family coat of arms, or occasionaly to add little sayings or verses. In most cases the pewterer did the engraving himself. It has often been worn away as the metal is so soft. Engraving was also used on prayer-tablets and sign-boards.

The examples we have of *wriggled-work* are far more numerous. The cutting tool is rocked to and fro, producing a zig-zag line, a considerably easier operation than engraving a straight line. The pattern drawn depends upon the speed of the movement and the width of the tool. This type of engraving, which is often seen on the familiar tumbler-shaped beakers, is revealed by close inspection.

Occasionally a design is made by *scratching-in* with a needle; this method is often mistaken for etching in wax. Etching is more suitable for hard metals, as it soon wears off pewter.

Chiseling-lines made with the aid of a hammer are sometimes found on pewter. They are produced by moving the chisel a fraction forward after each blow. In contrast with line engraving this method does not remove any of the metal, but it results in a similar flowing line.

In decorative work produced by *stamping*, designs are made or existing patterns framed by means of a die, or of several dies, applied in a fixed order.

Painting or lacquering pewter occurred particularly in the time of decadence, and was probably more suited to the furniture and interiors of that period. The painting was usually done on pewter of poor quality. This kind of ornamentation is seen on candlesticks, coffee pots, tobacco-boxes etc., made at the end of the 18th. and the beginning of the 19th. century. Sometimes designs were engraved in the lacquer.

Inlaid or applied copper was sometimes used as a means of decoration on pewter in Eastern Europe and Germany, but was seldom seen elsewhere. There is a rare specimen of this work, a flagon, in the Rijksmuseum in Amsterdam. A picture in the Provincial Museum in s'Hertogenbosch painted by an Antwerp master, called 'De Heeren van Lier', shows a few pewter flagons, some of the spouted type, clearly decorated with copper bands.

Pewter itself was used occasionally for inlaid or applied work, as on the wooden 'Pechkrug' tankards, on furniture and on relic-boxes. Tin-foil seems to have been used for decorating earthenware as far back as the time of the old French pile-dwellers.

Although pewter has been both decorated and been used for decorating purposes during many centuries, the craftsmen of Western Europe have not much indulged in ornamentation.

With us, the decoration of pewter was never forbidden, as it once was in the town of Geneva. But the beauty of the product was displayed by other means, more in keeping with the quality of the material. By the use of a good alloys, logical construction and honest workmanship.

We will not say that good pewter was made only in countries surrounding the North Sea, but we do contend that very little bad pewter was produced there.

The collector who believes that simplicity is the hall-mark of quality will appreciate the undeniable dignity of simple, undecorated pewter.

COLLECTORS AND COUNTERFEITERS

Quae nocent docent

JUST AS THE OUTER APPEARANCE of pewter-ware is simple, so the inner being of the collector is complicated. What sort of men join this queer group, and what inspires these odd people? They are possessed by a passion which is difficult to explain to those not sharing it, an enthusiasm aroused through various causes.

Of all the reasons which would urge one to be a collector, vanity is the worst, also the most stupid. For a snob will never attract more than a few spectators, among whom even fewer will have a sincere interest in his work, and an intelligent interest leaves him unmoved.

A less objectionable motive is the rarity of the specimens, which adds a zest to the hunt, and offers a more peaceful satisfaction than the pleasures of the chase with a gun.

The appreciation of the aesthetic value of the objects, as an impulse, probably deserves the highest esteem. We might say that a lover of art would look for objects which have been created solely for aesthetic or ideal motives. Pewter, however, even though as a rule it was made for practical purposes, also has its aesthetic appeal.

Some search for objects of historical value, while others are fascinated by the mystery of the unknown, hidden in their depths, which is often part of the charm of old things. Others collect for the cultural or folkloristic importance of the objects.

Scientific interest in the subject, such as a knowledge of the techniques employed, the material and styles, undoubtedly raises the level of the hobby. The apprentice pewter-collector cannot hope to rise to the rank of master until he has acquired something of the jargon of these people; the sometimes hardly justified terms such as the British 'Beefeater' flagons, the Dutch 'Rembrandt', 'Jan Steen' and 'Lambs' flagons, the 'Cardinal's hat' plates, the 'Loving-cups', the Scottish 'Tappit Hens,' the Irish 'Haystack' measures, etc., words which belong to the vernacular of the true collector.

It has been said that collecting pewter is a mild form of madness, for which there is only one remedy: more pewter. But without the activities of the collectors, where would the products of this noble craft be now?

Only lately has it been recognised how many beautiful things have been wrought out of this metal. In Holland, the Boymans Museum in Rotterdam has succeeded still in acquiring a large collection, but most other museums have missed the opportunity to obtain representative collections of the products of this craft, and now it is too late. In the antique shops they are practically no more to be found. There are of course a few good pieces here and there, in private or public possession, but collections which give a complete view of one aspect, or of the whole range of the pewterers work, are small in number.

What is the reason for this? Pewter does not suit the taste of those who find pleasure in creating an atmosphere of luxury by the display of costly porcelain and silver. Furthermore, whereas a heavy purse still goes a long way in buying precious objects at an auction, it goes less far these days when trying to buy the 'cheaper' pewter. One has to search with the divining rod of the hunter's instinct, and even then a really good piece is rarely tracked down.

There are still of course saltcellars and platters of little value to be found. A large number of these even turn out to be fakes. But the good specimens of the old hey-days have nearly all gone. At least there is nothing to be found without the use of diligence and knowledge.

These qualities are also needed to detect fakes.

Now that genuine pieces are rare, and therefore expensive, copying them is a remunerative business. The amount and variety of fakes have now reached fantastic proportions. They are made in two different ways. New pewter is given an antique appearance, or old pieces are altered by artful tricks so that they may be considered to belong in a higher category.

The path of the collector is not all strewn with roses: at first he will be pricked by many thorns, and these, the counterfeits, must be removed as soon as possible. Lost money should be regarded as the apprentice fee.

'We learn by our losses', and we can learn a great deal by

studying these fakes. A collector should also see as great a number of genuine specimens as possible, and examine them carefully, both in public and private collections, and in paintings. He should not be tempted to make a purchase in a hurry, and if he is doubtful about the authenticity of a piece he should leave it. Although people learn more from personal experience than from the advice of others, I would still like to mention a few salient points here.

It is generally advisable to acquire some knowledge of the old working methods of the craft, together with an idea of the different techniques used by the counterfeiters: thereby obtaining an over-all view of both fields. In the first place not too much value must be placed upon the marks or the style, as there are bona-fide pewter work-shops where copies of the old models are made, or who still possess and use the original moulds. These objects especially, are made antique later on by the fakers, and are sometimes even stamped with an imitation of the old marks. Attempts have been made to put a stop to this practice, by marking each piece with deeply incised stamps, as the usual relief marks can easily be ground away.

The two most commonly used methods of faking are the application of an artificial patina, and of artificial abrasions.

The artificial patina is usually greyer, and comes off more easily than a natural patina, when citric acid is used for example. A magnifying glass is a help in the detection of artificial wear and tear, as natural abrasions show softer edges than those produced by the use of a file or by sandpaper. In addition we must consider carefully, which part of the object has been in contact with the ground or a wall, or where the hand rubbed on it during use. For instance, regular handling has, in time, given the handle of a tankard a peculiar polish which is very difficult to imitate. The forger does not always add this effect or the signs of wear in the logical places. An unnatural absence of any marks of wear and tear might be explained by the salesman as due to little or cautious use. A 'cautious use' of his offer would be recommended. It must not be forgotten that ornamental pieces and domestic utensils will have a differing patina and degree of wear. The relief work on the authentic 'Edelzinn', for instance, is mostly very sharp and clear. Now and then it happens that the public give this sharpness a wrong interpretation at sales, and prefer to buy, instead, the blurry, faked specimens. This also applies, more or less, to objects which were in daily use. On the handles of old tankards one can often see the stroke of the scraper quite clearly, in spite of the wear caused by holding them in the hand. The artisans were most proficient in the way they handled their tools, and their products bear witness to the firm, fluent, unwavering hand which directed them. This is characterized by the direct, powerful thrust and stroke made by chisel or knife. As the execution of the work was exact, filing and scouring was, as a rule, unnecessary, and would have blurred the clear lines. This gives a genuine antique pewter specimen such a convincing look, when it is placed beside the flabby, saccharine, finicking counterfeit.

Under the lens, old pewter has a porous look. Fakers try to obtain this effect by beating the surface with a steel-wire brush (in Germany it is called 'gepeitschtes zinn': whipped pewter), but as a rule they overdo this process. As a matter of fact, this type of over-emphasis is an error by which many tricks betray themselves. Only a first class faker knows exactly when to stop. Naturally some knowledge of the technique of casting is important. As an example, the circular grooves produced by the lathe on the underside of dishes and inside flagons and tankards are finer and more regular on modern pieces than the distinct, but less clear-cut grooves on the old objects, which were made on the more primitive old lathe. On brightly polished old pewter, a dull patina is sometimes still visible in these furrows. Traces of tin pest are also difficult to imitate, but dents, cracks and saggings are easily faked.

Tricks are also played on antique pewter; hanging soapdishes are converted into 'monastery beakers' (and – mundus vult decipi – to crown the forgery the name of the monastery is added). Salts are changed into holy-water basins, and patens made from a saltcellar and a dish. We have already mentioned that new chasing is added to old dishes. On the rims of dishes imaginary coats of arms are engraved. This new engraving can generally be distinguished with the naked eye by its sharpness and ill contrived lines, and the style of engraving occasionally copies that of an earlier date than the piece itself. In the south of the

IX

Netherlands, old narrow-rimmed dishes are aged a few centuries by being repressed into 'Cardinal's hat' plates with broad rims. A close inspection of the back of the newly-formed wide rim reveals traces of the old narrow rim. In Germany 'Edelzinn' is in such demand that a great deal is frequently imitated there (the alloys used are often poor in tin, and the authentic sharpness of the decorative work is missing).

In Holland the demand for 'porringers' and a certain type of slender 'Rembrandt' tankard has created an abundant supply of imitations.

Mention of all the ingenuities practised in this field would be impossible, and indeed unnecessary; better than all the indications we can give are the patience and commonsense of the collector. Yet, even the most experienced connoisseur may find that he has been taken-in by a clever fake. If this fake is so deceptive as to resemble the genuine article exactly, should it not then be considered of equal value? In the case of the true collector, as long as this piece remains in his keeping it will be a source of irritation to him, since it is a fake. Besides this feeling of annoyance, defects in the material will come to light in the long run also. It is often said that the first impression is the right one. Perhaps this can be explained by the fact that, half unconsciously, we feel that the counterfeit lacks the good sound properties of the genuine example. An object created from a beautiful impulse usually awakens in others a thrill by its beauty, and it is not important whether the maker's impulse was realized in past ages or recently. An imitation is however mostly the result of quite different motives. It differs from the original in that the special combination of maker, material and technique cannot be repeated. If a craftsman of our time tries to take the place of an artisan of an earlier century, a sort of comedy is played, which is demonstrated in disharmony of the work produced. This lack of harmony is clearly revealed when the piece is placed among genuine examples. Even with objects made of such a simple material as pewter, the real thing shows strength and conviction, of which the imitation is found wanting.

Even in the humble but honest article of daily use, something of the maker, something personal, remains. This is one of its greatest charms for the collector, and one of the reasons why he sets out to acquire and maintain a collection.

Some attention must be given to the care of pewter also.

Repairs of antique pewter, at least of a more complicated nature, should be left to the expert craftsman. The soldering and other repair of partly decayed spots require special skill, and bad repair work may spoil a fine piece irremediably. For that reason an entirely unrestored object, 'straight from its mother' in the collectors lingo, is a most welcome addition to a collection. Small holes can be filled up with a moist rag held underneath, bigger ones must have a fitting piece of pewter soldered in. The solder used should have a lower melting-point than the plumbers' ordinary solder, and a really expert mend can hardly be traced. A crack can be soldered more easily if it is not too old and dirty, but in any case the part to be mended must first be well cleaned. Pieces which have been patched up by indifferent workmanship should not be included in a collection, and each object must be complete. Meanwhile all kinds of dents and scratches can be improved by a capable hand, and there is no reason why this should not be done. Vexing scratches can be removed with a piece of very fine sand-paper and then a little polishing; small scratches with polishing alone. Dents must be carefully rubbed away or pressed out, with a blunt wooden handle for example. They should not be hammered unless a thin metal sheet is set between as a buffer. If a small piece has to be inserted in the rim of a lid or dish, a plaster-cast should first be made from a sound piece.

In most cases cleaning can be done at home. If in the course of years a beautiful dark patina is formed—a natural patina develops slowly, being the lustre of the ages—it is better not to remove it, but to enhance its beauty by polishing it with a little wax, particularly when the object concerned is not in use. On pieces of pewter-ware which have been dredged up, we sometimes find a patina of a peculiar golden colour, which can also be intensified with a little wax polish. It is useless to polish pewter with a high lead content, as the colour will always remain dull and cannot be improved. Polishing 'Edelzinn' may cause the relief work to wear off. When a dirty surface has been cleaned, the lustre will remain mellow, and the charm of the antique need not be lost. Dirt should be removed, but not the fine patina.

Scouring is the quickest way of cleaning bright pewter, but since this method scratches, the surface does not obtain the deep dark sheen. If it is done, then the movement must be in one direction, straight or in circles. A harmless method for the removal of the unwished-for layer of dirt collected through the ages, is to hang the object for some time in slowly boiling water containing hay, or soaking it in paraffin. It seldom happens for a piece to be so thoroughly corroded, that it is no longer possible to clean it.

A small amount of metal polish, and then fine chalk and oil, are quite good for the upkeep of pewter with no patina. According to Welch, the London pewterers appointed someone to oil the pewter in the Guildhall regularly. A thin layer of vaseline can also be used as a protective coating, and warm soap-suds are sufficient for regular cleaning. It is not advisable to use sharp acids for cleaning (though vinegar is harmless). They cause a roughness on the surface and make it turn an ugly aluminium colour. Sand and abrasive paper should not be used as they inevitably scratch the metal. Very fine emery-powder or ground pumice would be better. Here also patience achieves the best results. An old and well-tried method is to use wood-ashes with a little pewter-wort.

Although it is certain that pewter was scoured and polished in olden times, it is strange that painters usually depicted it in dark tones of blue and black, making it look as if it already had a patina. Should we conclude from this that scouring was not so common as is generally supposed, or was it traditional to use this colour in painting pewter to contrast it more sharply with silver? If it was only discolouration of the paint or varnish due to the passing of years, the pictures would have told us this after they had been cleaned. The primitives did not trouble much about obtaining the special pewter colour, but the painters of the 16th. and 17th. centuries seem to have paid a great deal of attention to this metal, while on pictures of the 18th. century pewter is rarely seen.

The 'beginner' collector may safely start on the care of his collection himself. When polishing a newly acquired antique cabinet, we soon discover which parts have been repaired or restored. It is the same with pewter; by handling the objects one gets to know them. During an examination, the hands (weight, flexibility and sound) are often as important as the eyes. It stands to reason that undamaged pewter pieces, like furniture, become more rare, the earlier the period to which they belong.

We have already admitted that the satisfaction of having obtained an object just because it is rare, is not the noblest quality in the psychology of the collector. But the difficulties encountered sometimes make it an adventurous and exciting sport.

The rarity of the object need not be a reason to treat it as a wonder of the world. The humble metal from which it is made has no intrinsic value. It was used for making simple utensils, which do not feel quite at home in a showcase or at an exhibition.

Pewter is even less at home among precious porcelain and brittle knick-knacks, or against a floral wallpaper. Tankards and flagons feel out of place on lace table centres, on mahogany, or on a highly polished poudreuse. Shyly and reproachfully they look at you from a richly gilt table or beside a pompous silver candelabra. Set them among more congenial company, on an oak chest or cupboard, beside an earthen-ware bowl or jug. Place them on the bold red of a Persian carpet, or against the shining white of a stucco wall.

Pewter smiles upon us like a child, unselfconsciously. Pewter sings a simple melody, so give it no great accompaniment. Pewter does not belong in the strong-room or behind glass. It should stand free and near enough to be within reach of eyes and hands, and when possible be in convivial use. It asks for homely, intimate and harmonious surroundings. In a less kindly disposed environment it may find support in the presence of a few comrades, though in general they should not be placed too closely or in too great a number together. A specimen gains in expressiveness if somewhat isolated. Only then will pewter tell you the old tales of which it is full. Monotony there need not be in the collectors room, for there are tints on the antique beakers and tankards varying from the brightest silver-lustre to patinas of the deepest black.

Which metal shows so much change of surface, so many moods of colour and so much variety of form?

Perhaps you will now admit that pewter was used for more than the clumsy implements of digestion, the plate, the porringer, the chubby chamber-pot.

Perhaps you too, will prefer at times some gaiety to stateliness, the tankard to soberness, pleasure to business.

Perhaps you will then realise as I did, that pewter-ware is not inferior to silver.

Then you will understand why I wanted to drink once more to the age-worn, yet kind and familiar face of old pewter.

BIBLIOGRAPHY

Periodicals

K. Azijnman
De achttien oude wijnkannen der Illustre Lieve Vrouwen Broederschap te 's Hertogenbosch, Oude Kunst, deel IV, 1918/19, blz. 20.
De Gilde-kannen in het stedelijk Museum te Nijmegen, Oudheidkundig Jaarboek, 1925, blz. 48.

Prof. E. Cohen
Tinpest en museumziekte, de Ingenieur, Jaargang XXIII, 1918, blz. 529.
Zelfde onderwerp in Natuur en Techniek, September 1931, blz. 206.

B. de Kock
Twee 15e-eeuwsche Rotterdamsche tinnen bakjes, Oud Nederland, 1950, afl. 8, blz. 7.
Stille getuigen van de Overwintering op Nova Zembla, Oud Nederland, 1950, afl. 8, blz. 15.

J. Kruizinga
In de Werkplaats van de Tinnegieters, Hobby, April 1949, blz. 110.

Dr H. M. R. Leopold
De rol van het tin in de geschiedenis van de oud-Grieksche beschaving, Mededeelingen van het Ned. Hist. Instituut Rome, 1927.

D. F. Lunsingh Scheurleer
De Tinnen stadskannen in Nederland, Oudheidkundig Jaarboek 1940, afl. I, blz. 15.
Tin op Schilderijen, Oud Nederland, 1950, afl. 8, blz. 1.

Mr W. G. D. Murray
De Rotterdamsche Tinnegieters, Rotterdamsch Jaarboekje, 1938, blz. 1—32.

J. G. N. Renaud
Iets over tinmerken, Oudheidkundig Jaarboek, September 1944, blz. 7.

M. A. de Visser
Drie Groningsche Hanze-tin kannen, Oud Nederland, 1950, afl. 8, blz. 11.

Dr A. Wassenbergh
Het oude Tinnegietersbedrijf in Friesland, de Vrije Fries, 1943.

R. M. Vetter and H. H. Cotterel
Various articles in "Antiques", Boston, "International Studio", New York, "Apollo", London.

Boncoud	L'Orfèvrerie d'étain français, Art et Industrie XIII, 1948.
Adolphe Riff	Deux artisans alsaciens du XVIIe siècle, Archives Alsaciennes d'histoire de l'Art III, 1924.
Dr Gust Bossard	Schweizer Zinnkannen, Beilage zum Jahrbuch S. A. C., Bern 1908.
K. Kratzenberger	Altes norddeutsches Zinngerät und seine Marken, Charlottenburg.
Prof. O. Lauffer	Spätmittelalterliche Zinnfunde aus Hamburg, Mitteilungen aus dem Museum für Hamburgische Geschichte, 1912.
G. Mirow	Der Müllroser Zinnfund. Mitt. des Ver. für Heimatkunde d. Kr. Lebus, Bd. II, H. 1, 1916.
O. Pniower	Mittelalterliche Zinnkannen aus dem Mark Brandenburg, Brandenburgia, XXV Jahrgang.
Fr. von Rziha	Böhmische Zinngefasse, Mitteilungen der Zentralkommission zur Erhaltung der Kunstdenkmale, Bd. XVIII, S. 27, 1982.

Books

Jos de Beer	Bedevaart- en pelgrimsplaatjes, Gedenkboek Frans Claes Museum, Antwerp.
Mr W. F. H. Oldewelt	Het Tinnegietersgilde, Amsterdamsche Archiefvondsten, 1942, blz. 80.
J. G. N. Renaud	Oude Ambachtskunst, 1943, blz. 53.
A. J. G. Verster	Oud Tin, 1924, 2e ed. 1928.
	Tin door de eeuwen, 1954, 2e ed. 1957
Malcolm Bell	Old Pewter, London, 1913.
R. M. Vetter and H. H. Cotterel	European Continental Pewter, 1927.
H. H. Cotterel	National types of Old Pewter, 1925.
	Old Pewter, its makers and marks in England, Scotland and Ireland, 1929.
	Pewter down the ages, 1932.
E. J. Gale	Pewter and the amateur collector, 1910.
L. Ingleby Wood	Scottish Pewterware and Pewterers ,1905.
C. A. Markham	Pewter marks and old Pewterware, 1909, 2nd ed. 1928.
H. J. L. Massé	Pewter Plate, London, 2nd ed., 1910.
	Chats on old Pewter, 1911, 2nd ed. 1949.
	The Pewter collector, 1921.
Ronald F. Michaelis	Antique Pewter of the British Isles, London, 1955.

A. de Navarro	Causeries on English Pewter, 1911.
Charles Welsh	History of the Worshipful Company of Pewterers of the City of London, 1902.
G. Bapst	Etudes sur l'Etain dans l'antiquité et et au moyen âge, 1884.
	L'étain, Paris, 1888.
M. Dufréné	Etude sur l'histoire de la production et du commerce de l'Etain, 1881.
H. Havard	Dictionnaire de l'Ameublement, 1887—1890, p. 524.
E. Naef	L'Etain et le livre du Potier d'étain genevois, 1920.
Ad. Riff	L'orfèvrerie d'Etain en France.
	Les Ecuelles à Bouillon, 1925.
	Les aiguières en Casque, 1926.
	Les étains Strasbourgeois, 1925.
Salmon	Art du potier d'étain, 1788.
Fardy	Les étains Français, Paris.
K. Berling	Altes Zinn, Bibliothek für Kunst- und Antiquitäten-Sammler, 1919.
	Stadtmarken Sächsischer Zinngieszer, 1913.
Dr Gust. Bossard	Die Zinngieszer der Schweiz und ihr Werk, 1920.
H. Demiani	François Briot, Caspar Enderlein und das Edelzinn, Leipzig, 1897.
Fr. Fischer	Böhmisches Zinn und seine Marken, 1928.
J. Gahlnbäck	Zinn und Zinngieszer in Liv-, Est- und Kurland, 1929.
	Russisches Zinn, 1928.
Erwin Hintze	Nürnberger Zinn, 1921.
	Die Deutschen Zinngieszer und ihre marken, 1921/27.
U. Huber und G. Oertel	Siebenbürgisch, Sächsisches und anderes Zinn, 1936.
W. Reinicke	Lüneburger Zinn, 1947.
J. Warncke	Die Zinngieszer zu Lübeck, 1922.
G. Wolfbauer	Die Steirischen Zinngieszer und ihre Marken, 1934.
A. Löfgren	Det Svenska Tenngjutarehantverkets Historia. Stockholm, 1933.

Exhibitions and Collections

's-Gravenhage Museum	H. C. Gallois, Catalogus Tintentoonstelling Gemeente Museum, 1925.

Leiden Museum   Tentoonstelling museum "de Lakenhal", 1927.

Zutphen Museum   Tentoonstelling, 1938.

Delft Museum   Tentoonstelling museum "Prinsenhof", 1950.

Dr R. Forrer   Les Etains de la collection Alfred Ritling, 1905.

Zinn- Cimelien der Sammlung Hofrath Kahlbau, Straszburg, 1908.

Karl Schaefer   Die Sammlung W. Clemens, Kunstgewerbe Museum der Stadt Köln, 1923.

A. von Walcher Moltheim   Deutsches und Französisches Edelzinn aus zwei Wiener Sammlungen (Dr Figdor und Graf Wilzeck), Kunst und Kunsthandwerk IX, S. 65, 1904.

Sammlung Dr A. Figdor   Auktion Cassirer, Tl. I, 1930.

Sammlung Prof. Adolf Hengeler   Auktion Helbing, 1931.

Sammlung Carl Nestel   Auktion Helbing, 1916.

For publications concerning regional pewter-ware see also the above mentioned works by Massé, Berling, Demiani.

NOTES ON THE ILLUSTRATIONS

3. Flasks, otherwise known as 'pilgrim-bottles'. Thick-walled. The two ears serve for belting. On the right, flask with so-called 'ploughshare' base, XVth century. The other two about 1500. Height from right to left: 10¹/₂ in., 8¹/₂ in., 9¹/₂ in.

4. Flasks. Above, ornament consists of a scooped out centre, edged with foliage motif in relief. H. 6¹/₂ in. The other two show hunting scenes in relief. Flask on right of Balkan origin, H. 5¹/₂ in.; on left Persian, H. 9 in. The figure of the horseman on the latter has presumably been adapted from the Nuremberg 'Gustav Adolf' plate.

5. Chamber pots. XVIth century. H. 4¹/₂ in. - 6 in.

6. Measures. Cast in two vertical sections. XVIth century. Height, from right to left: 4 in., 5¹/₂ in., 6 in.

7. Measures. XVIIth and XVIIIth century. The largest marked Bremen. H. 4¹/₂ in., the smaller 2 in. - 2¹/₂ in. Some stamped with gauges.

8. Measure and flask. XVIIth century. Measure stamped with gauge. H. 10 in., touch: Flask and Castle (Flushing and Middelburg), initialled L. H.

9. Gothic octagonal flagon. French(?). (Similar specimens: in the Rijksmuseum, Amsterdam; Landes Museum, Zürich, originally from Aargau; Victoria & Albert Museum, London; the collection of Mr. M. Meyer, Paris). XIVth century. H. 8¹/₂ in.

10. Flagon shaped as flask. Reinforced on two sides with heart-shaped shields. Similar specimen in the Kunst-gewerbe Museum, Cologne. Early XVth century. H. 6¹/₂ in. House-mark.

11. Large flagon with relief-ornamented handle. Cast in two vertical sections. Single hinge. Religious medallions in lid and bottom. Anno 1331. H. 6¹/₂ in.

12. Medallion on lid of the 'Hanseatic' XIVth century flagon reproduced in illustration 11.

13. Flagon. Cast in two vertical halves. Single hinge. Handle in Gothic style; thumbpiece in the form of a hammer. Later XVth century. H. 8¹/₂ in. House-mark.

14. Flagon cast in two vertical sections, single hinge, relief-

ornamented handle. Hamburg(?). Bottom-seal. XVth century. H. 10 in.

15. Flagon on wide base. Cast in two vertical sections, single hinge. XVIth century. H. 7 in.

16. Flagon. Cast in two vertical sections, single hinge. Medallion on bottom. Rouen(?). XVIth century. H. 6 in.

17. Flagons. Cast in two vertical sections. Single hinges. Second half of XVIth century. From right to left: Leyden, H. $7^1/_2$ in.; Mechelen, H. $8^1/_2$ in.; Hoorn, H. 8 in. Each marked with the arms of the city of origin.

18. Flagons. Gauge stamp on rim indicating they have been used as measures. On right: single hinge, XVIth century, H. $5^1/_2$ in., marked with the arms of Rotterdam, Rose mark, T.W. On left: double hinge, XVIIth century, H. $3^1/_2$ in., Rose mark.

19. Tankards. On left: single hinge, bottom-seal, coin inside lid, XVIth century. The other two about 1600. Centre: single hinge, bottom-seal, marked with the arms of Leyden. H. 4 - $4^1/_2$ in.

20. Tankards. On right, with single hinge, Rotterdam, early XVIth century. H. $4^1/_2$ in., Gothic A. The other two about 1600. The tankard in centre, single hinge, on high foot, shows signs of 'tin-pest' sickness. H. 6 in. and $4^1/_2$ in.

21. Flagon. Gouda, late XVIth century. The golden-black patina of this dredged up piece has unfortunately been removed and is now only discernable on its underside. H. $6^1/_2$ in. Marked with the arms of the city.

22. Flagon. Late XVIIth century. Measuring peg affixed inside. H. $10^1/_2$ in., marked Rose.

23. Flagon. Amsterdam. XVIIth century. H. 12 in. Marked with the arms of the city.

24. Flagon and miniature flagon. Amsterdam. Late XVIIth century, H. $9^1/_2$ in. and $4^1/_2$ in. Marked with the arms of the city.

25. Two miniature flagons. Late XVIth century. Smallness emphasized by silhouette of large flagon in background. Flagon on right fashioned on ceramic lines. H. $3^1/_2$ in., Rose, P. B. On left: type of so-called 'Council' flagon. H. $4^1/_2$ in.

26. Small jugs. Smallness emphasized by silhouette of large flagon in background. Right: XVIth century, single hinge, H. 5¹/₂ in., house-mark. The other three early XVIIth century, gauge stamps. From right to left: H. 2¹/₂ in., Rose, A. V. F.; H. 5¹/₂ in., Rose, A. D. F.; H. 4 in.

27. Measures. On right: the Hague, XVIIth century, H. 4¹/₂ in., marked with the arms of the town. Centre: Amsterdam, XVIIth century, H. 3 in., marked with the arms of the city. On left: high-footed burette, late XVIth century, H. 4 in.

28. Burettes for water and wine. Above: two XVIIIth century burettes on Louis XV tray. Below: two XVIIth century. H. 4 in. - 5¹/₂ in.

29. Spouted flagons. On right: single hinge, with spout reaching to base. XVIth century, H. 5¹/₂ in., marked with the arms of Haarlem, Gothic D. On left: double hinge, so-called 'Lamb's' flagon. XVIIth century. H. 4¹/₂ in., Rose, I. H.

30. Spouted flagons and tankards. XVIIth century. From right to left: French (Toulouse), H. 7 in.; Swiss (unlike the Dutch so-called 'Jan Steen' flagon, the spout of the Swiss flagon has a connecting bar), marked with the arms of the city of Freibourg, Lion and Keys, C. W. F., H. 10 in.; Flemish, H. 4¹/₂ in., Rose, G. V. I.; Hungarian, handle relief-decorated, H. 5¹/₂ in.

31. Guild flagon. Dutch. Drinking vessel of the Shoemakers Guild. Inscription in block letters and italics, engraved ornament. XVIIIth century. H. 10 in., marked Rose.

32. Guild flagon (Zutphen), two miniature flagons and ewer. The guild flagon has an inscription on the lid in italics, 'Schippersgilt, Gerrit Janssen Mastoverboord, 1700'. H. 10 in., marked Rose, I. K. R. (Roelofsen).

33. Tankard. Originally belonging to a local community. Vertical lines, achieved by scraping, in centre section enhance decorative effect. Foliage ornamented border on both sides. Lid engraved in block letters: The residents of Wilsem. Dated 1593. H. 9 in., marked Rose.

34. Large Guild flagon. Cologne. Dated 1689. Engraved

with lengthy presentation inscription, names of members of the Guild are inscribed in a laurel wreath. H. 13½ in.

35. Tankard. Nuremberg. Arabesque ornament in relief. Cast from an engraved mould. Made by Jacob Koch II (1572—1619), pupil of Nicolaus Horchheimer and colleague of Enderlein. Touch: Hammer, S. S., H. 7½ in.

36. Swiss jug and two German jugs. On right: Basle, made by Nicolas Ubeli, chased ornament decoration, ceramic form. First half of the XVIIIth century. H. 6 in. Centre: guild jug, so-called 'Rörcken', dated 1645, H. 7 in. On left: relief-ornament garden of Eden scene. Saxony, early XVIIth century, H. 6 in.

37. German guild pieces. On right: Nuremberg, with bronze tap. Butchers' Guild. Dated 1669. H. 22 in. On left: goblet, so-called 'Wilkomm' (Welcome), with silver shields of the masters attached. The female figure original- ly had a banner in her hand. Carpenters' Guild. Dated 1716. H. 17½ in.

38. French wine flagon. Origin Champagne, one hinged handle and one fixed, so-called 'Cymaise'. About 1600. H. 12 in.

39. Ewer (for Communion service?), fashioned on classical lines. Ornament in relief. Late XVIth century. H. 10 in.

40. Ewer and basin. Relief-ornamented, early XVIIIth century, H. 8 in., Angel mark.

41. Two dishes with narrow rim. Above: diameter 9 in., below: diameter 13 in. Four small plates with raised centres. About 6 in. in diameter. First half of XVIth century.

42. Flat plate with narrow upraised rim, modelled on the lines of a wooden trencher. Diameter 7 in., touch C. G. Porringers with one and two ears, such as seen in Jan Mostaert's painting of the Holy Family (frontispiece), H. 4½ in., marked with the arms of Rotterdam, XVIth century.

43. Porringers. Of the two smallest, the one below is early XVIth century. One-eared type which has also been used for wine tasting. Diameter 5½ in. The small porringer above dates from the second half of the XVIth century,

diamter 4¹/₂ in., marked with Gothic Y. Of the two large porringers, the one below is of XVIIth century. Diameter 9 in. The top one has two differing ears and can be hung on a wall. About 1700. Diameter 10 in.

44. Wine flagon with ring handle and lid on spout. Munich. XVIIIth century, H. 9 in.; Flemish one-eared drinking bowl. XVIIIth century; Friesian drinking bowl with two ears. Ornament in relief and engraving, early XVIIth century, diameter 4 in.

45. One large and five diminutive so-called 'Cardinal's Hat' dishes. XVIIth century. Diameter of large dish is 21 in. Marked Rose and the arms of Antwerp. Small dishes 1¹/₂ - 4¹/₂ in.

46. Dish with flat, broad rim. Flemish, XVIIth century, 10 in. diameter. Marked at the back, Rose, D. H. (Daniel Huysman) and with the arms of Antwerp.

47. Very large dish hammered out of a sheet of pewter. The hammer-work also serves as decoration. Probably produced as a test specimen for promotion to mastership. Diameter 25 in.

48. Dishes with broad rim, so-called 'Cardinal's Hat' dishes. XVIIth century. On right: dated 1660, H. G.; centre: Rose and Angel marks, P. V. B.; on left: Rose mark and the arms of Antwerp. H. 12¹/₂ in., 18 in., 22 in.

49. Tray, 13¹/₂ in. × 17¹/₂ in. Set of six plates, diameter 8 in., marked with X and Crown., Counterfeit silver hall-marks., F. v. d. Bogaert. Style Louis XIV.

50. Various types of engraved ornamentation. The large tray made by hammering a pewter sheet, marked in centre I. H. S. with angels engraved on two sides. Early XVIIIth century. From right to left: I. 12¹/₂ in. × 15¹/₂ in., marked Rose and the arms of Antwerp, Daniel Huysman; II. Diameter 8¹/₂ in.; III. Diameter 6¹/₂ in., Angel mark, H. A. W.

51. Large dish. So-called 'Edelzinn' ('noble pewter'). Ornamentation etched by the master-pewterer, Nicolaus Horchheimer, on the bronze mould in which dish was cast, a process producing shallow relief as opposed to the ornamentation in high relief produced from engraved

moulds. Nuremberg, XVIth century. Diameter 15^1/$_2$ in., N. H.

52. Large ornamented dish, so-called 'Temperantia' dish. Ornament in high relief, engraved on bronze mould by C. Enderlein. Dish cast by his colleague Jacob Koch II. On back a medallion with the portrait of the master-pewterer; on rim inscription: 'Sculpebat Casbar Enderlein'. Early XVIIth century. Diameter 18 in.

53. Plates with ornament in high relief. 'Edelzinn'. Representation in centre: Noah's thanksgiving. On the rim, garden of Eden. Nuremberg. Early XVIIth century. Initialled by the mould engraver, Paulus Oham der Altere, and showing caster's emblem, a halved eagle, P. O. Diameter 7 in.

54. Large dish, 'Seder-dish'. Engraving depicting Jewish Passover meal. On rim inscription in Hebrew. XVIIIth century. Diameter 17^1/$_2$ in., Rose, I. T.

55. German beer tankards. XVIIIth century. On right so-called 'pitch tankard', made of wood, the inside covered with a layer of pitch, outside inlaid pewter ornament. H. 6 in. Left: Wood covered with plaited reed. H. 6 in.

56. Drinking vessel in the form of a shell. XVIIIth century. H. 6 in.

57. Five beakers. XVIIth and XVIIIth century. Above, so-called 'Communion beaker', with line engraving. H. 7 in. Right, beaker on foot, wriggled work, French, H. 4^1/$_2$ in. On right below, one of the rare specimens of relief-ornamented Dutch pewter, H. 2^1/$_2$ in.

58. Small beakers. XVIth and XVIIth century. Probably used for measuring out sailors' rum ration. The beaker in the background is shown for the purpose of comparing sizes. H. 1 in. - 2^1/$_2$ in.

59. Five drinking bowls (the smallest ones presumably measures). XVIth and XVIIth century. On right below, relief-ornament on handle, H. 4 in., others about 2 in. high.

60. Salts. XVth and XVIth century. H. 1^1/$_2$ in. - 4 in.

61. Mustard-pot (?), H. 6 in. Two salts, H. 3^1/$_2$ in. and 4 in. About 1600.

62. Louis XIV table ware. Candlestick, H. 3 in., under the foot head of Christ. Milkjug, H. 4^1/$_2$ in. Mustard-pot, H. 3 in.

63. Louis XV table ware. Large tureen, H. 12 in. Two sugar bowls, H. 4 in. On the right, the ornament is cast from mould, on the left, chased line ornament.

64. Louis XVI table ware. Pepper-caster, H. 6 in. Sugar bowl, H. 4 in., relief-ornamented.

65. Tobacco boxes. Presumably originally lacquered. Provided with leaden pressers for pressing down the tobacco. From right to left: Louis XIV, marked Angel and X with Crown. Louis XIV, counterfeit silver hall-marks, Louis XV (Régence), marked 'Engels gepolijst harttin', counterfeit silver hall-marks. H. 7 in. - 8 in.

66. Tureen (Lubeck?), presumably property of an angler, H. 5^1/$_2$ in. Small tureen, H. 4 in. Butter-cooler, H. 3 in. Early XVIIIth century.

67. Condiment box, early XVIIIth century, H. 6 in. Two salts or condiment stands; on right, pierced work ornament, on left, relief-ornamented. H. 2 in. - 2^1/$_2$ in.

68. Louis XV table ware. Ladle, sieve, salt, sugar-bowl with spoon rack. German. Sugar-bowl H. 6 in., salt 2 in.

69. Monteith or 'wine cooler'. Early XVIIIth century, H. 8^1/$_2$ in.

70. Bell with ornament in relief. French. XVIIth century. H. 6 in.

71. Pestle and mortar. XVIIth century. H. 3^1/$_2$ in.

72. Spoons. One above with arched handle, XVth century. Set of six, early XVIIth century. Length 6 in.

73. Inkstand and box. XVIIth century. The inkstand with sand caster and drawer, engraved throughout. H. 3 in. Box with lion on sliding lid. H. 2 in.

74. Articles with painted ornament. Tray, diameter 12 in., tea-pot H. 8 in.; inkstand with drawer and sand caster, Louis XIV, H. 4 in.; toy set Louis XVI, H. 2 in. - 4 in.

75. Guild properties with engraved ornament. Above, Millers' Guild emblem, H. 13^1/$_2$ in. Below, Shoemakers' Guild drinking vessel. German. XVIIth century. H. 4^1/$_2$ in.

76. Chandelier for candles. Engraved ornament. XVIIth century.
77. Pricket candlestick, with iron pricket not fixed on grease-tray but at bottom of shaft. XIVth century. H. $5^1/_2$ in.
78. Church candlestick. About 1500. H. 9 in.
79. Church candlestick. Late XVIth century. H. $7^1/_2$ in.
80. Collar candlestick. Bad restoration on socket is clearly visible. Similar candlesticks, originally used by the Heemskerk and Barendsz Nova Zembla expedition, are in the Rijksmuseum, Amsterdam. Early XVIIth century. H. $8^1/_2$ in.
81. Collar candlestick and oil lamp. Mid-XVIIth century. H. $4^1/_2$ in. and 6 in.
82. Candlesticks. Early-, mid-, and late XVIIIth century. Style Louis XIV, Louis XV, Louis XVI. H. $9^1/_2$ in., $7^1/_2$ in., 10 in.
83. Large bracket candlestick. XVIIth century. Length 20 in.
84. Hanging oil lamps. H. 6 in. and $5^1/_2$ in. Snuffers, length 6 in.
85. Jewish Sabbath lamp with grease-tray. Early XVIIIth century. H. $15^1/_2$ in.
86. Jewish Maccabean lamp. Eight oil lamps, the ninth above is used for lighting the others. Holland. XVIIIth century. H. $10^1/_2$ in. Marked with 'X' and Crown, I. D. K., Lion, Angel, crowned head with stars.
87. Lavabo. Iron handle. XVIth century. H. $5^1/_2$ in.
88. Church utensils. XVIIth century. On the right, ciborium, the cup silver-plated on the inside, H. $13^1/_2$ in. On left, aspersorium, H. $4^1/_2$ in., and sprinkler.
89. Chalices. On right, chalice with paten, second half of the XVIth century, H. 7 in. Left below, hexagon shaped shaft, relief-ornamented on foot. First half of the XVIth century, H. 7 in. Left above, XIVth century, H. 4 in.
90. Diminutive chalices. XVth and XVIth century. Large chalice shown for the purpose of comparing sizes. H. $1^1/_2$ in. - $3^1/_2$ in.
91. Chrismatories containing one, two and three wells for consecrated oils. XVIth, XVIIth and XVIIIth century. H. $1^1/_2$ in. - $3^1/_2$ in.

92. Chrismatories. Containing removable wells to hold consecrated oils, lids provided with anointing sticks. XVIIth century. H. 4 in. - $5^1/_2$ in. One on right marked F. Angers.
93. Altar vase, H. 8 in. Bénitier, $2^1/_2$ in. XVIIIth century.
94. Bénitiers. XVIIIth century. H. 9 in.
95. Bénitier and pyxis. Bénitier on three claw feet, flat at back, with lion on lid. XVth century, H. $4^1/_2$ in. Pyxis on three lion feet, top with embattled edge, Gothic cruciferous flower. XVth century. H. $5^1/_2$ in.
96. Crucifix. Pewter on wood. Russian (?). H. 6 in.
97. Toys: spoon rack with spoons, coffee set and drinking set. XVIIIth century.
98. XVIIth and XVIIIth century toys. Shown on large hammered dish.
99. Toy plates with coloured food-stuff. XVIIIth century. Snuff boxes, vinaigrettes etc., XVIIIth century.
100. Village, painted pewter.
101. Toy plates with ornament in relief. Most of the articles shown on this and the following pages have been recovered from river beds.
102. Miniature table ware and kitchen ware, relief-ornamented.
103. Pilgrims' flutes, buttons, clasps. Pilgrims' ampullae for carrying relics from pilgrimages.
104. Religious objects, inter alia pilgrims' bells.
105. Pilgrims' badges with religious representations brought from pilgrimages. Sacred figures and other pilgrims' objects.
106. Crucifixes, ring and pilgrims' horn.
107. Religious statues. This pewter contains a large proportion of lead.

ILLUSTRATIONS

49

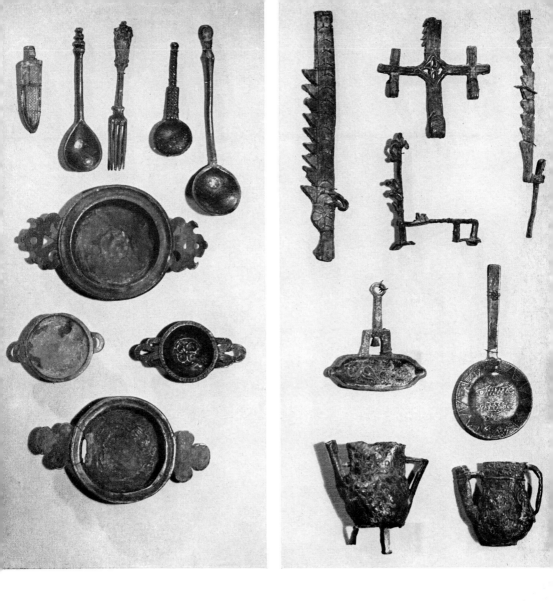

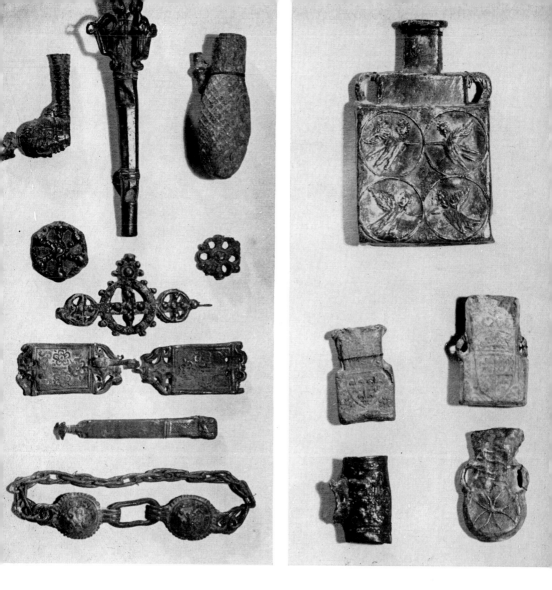